JAN '98

World Link

An Internet Guide for
Educators, Parents, and Students

Linda C. Joseph

ORIGINAL WORKS
GREYDEN PRESS, COLUMBUS, OHIO

World Link   An Internet Guide for Educators, Parents, and Students

Revised September 1995

ISBN 1-57074-244-8

http://www.smartpages.com/worldlink/worldlink.html

Printer/ Binder: Greyden Press, Columbus, Ohio.

"Cyberspace .... the endless frontier"

Cyber Bee

Acknowledgments

Karen Schwab, my "gopher" and good friend.

Dr. A. J. Miller for giving me my first Internet account.

Dr. Michael Burke for supporting my vision.

Brenda Gonzalez for her daily encouragement.

My daughter Michele for suggesting we get a second phone line.

Also Debbie Abilock of The Nueva School for permission to include their Acceptable Use Policy.

Meckler Publishing for permission to use the basic form for citing electronic resources.

Dr. Michael Eisenberg for the use of his Big Six Skills chart, definitions, and lesson plan form.

M. F. Schwab & Associates for the *Cover Design*
Robert Gallant for the *Graphic Illustration*
Steve Brady for the *Electronic Illustration*

TABLE OF CONTENTS

FOREWORD

World Link was a dream which originated nearly ten years ago, before all the publicity about Internet and the Information Superhighway. At that time the project was called Link to the World and it involved connecting to a few library subscription services with a 300 baud modem and an Apple IIe computer. The modem was slow and the services were not very user friendly to students or teachers.

In the Spring of 1992, a university professor offered me an Internet account if in return I would send him e-mail each week about my Internet exploration. For the next few months, without any sort of manual, I stumbled through the commands and figured out how to navigate the Internet. To this professor I am deeply indebted.

After cruising down the information highway, it became apparent there was a place for the Internet in the K-12 curriculum. But how would I coax my colleagues to use it? Writing a training manual seemed like a good idea, but the instructions had to be step-by-step and user friendly. Hands-on instruction and dissemination were also essential. With support from the Martha Holden Jennings Foundation, the first edition of this book was written.

This second edition of *World Link* is meant to be a living document. The monthly newsletter of the same name compliments the book by pointing to current projects and providing information about new resources. *World Link* is designed to grow with you as you continue to expand your knowledge of the Internet.

L.C.J.

The Information Superhighway

The Information Superhighway is a global network of networks connected by high speed telephone lines. These telephone lines allow data to be sent from one computer to another in a matter of seconds. The Internet is comprised of federal and state networks, universities, businesses, organizations, and K-12 schools. Created by the Department of Defense in 1969 as a network for communications, originally called ARPANET, it has evolved into a large network for government and educational research.

What makes the Internet an exciting avenue for elementary and secondary education is the unbelievable amount of information available and the opportunity to communicate with others. You can access electronic newsletters, text files, computer programs, graphics, computer development codes, databases, e-mail, and library catalogs around the world.

Educators: The advantages for educators are the ability to share ideas with colleagues, create and participate in projects, and access information from hundreds of resources.

Parents: The advantages for parents include the ability to communicate with teachers and other parents and share the learning experience with their children.

Students: The advantages for students are the ability to communicate with peers and mentors, search databases for research, share their projects, and learn problem-solving skills.

However, the most compelling reason to introduce the Internet into the classroom along with other technologies is that the expanding global economy will demand that employees be proficient in computer and information access skills.

While attending a conference in San Francisco, I stayed on the seventeenth floor of a large hotel. Each morning I peered out the window, and watched people heading for their jobs in the high-rise office buildings in the surrounding area. As the lights came on, I could see the layout of each office. It was an observation I won't forget. There on each desk was a computer workstation. My friend came over to the window and I said to her, "Look at each of those offices. They all have computers. How are we going to prepare our kids for the future if we don't have this same kind of technology in our schools?"

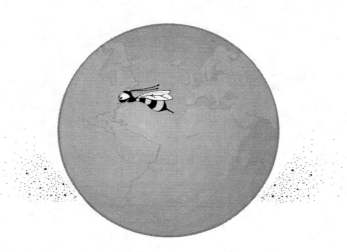

CHAPTER 1

Connection
Options

Internet Connection

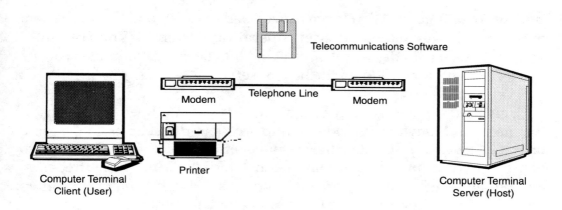

Telecommunications Software

Modem   Telephone Line   Modem

Printer

Computer Terminal
Client (User)

Computer Terminal
Server (Host)

Computers at different locations can communicate with each other when they are connected by a telephone line and a translator box called a modem. Information or data is sent over the telephone line in the form of electronic signals called bits. The modem translates these bits so that the computers are speaking the same language.

In order to make a basic online connection with another computer, the following equipment is needed: computer workstation with printer, standard telephone line, a modem (9600 baud or higher is best), and a telecommunications software program to run on the computer.

Full Internet access that includes e-mail, FTP, telnet, gopher, and other useful tools can be obtained in a variety of ways: dial-up, SLIP or PPP, or direct connection or node. Dial-up is simply using a modem, telephone line and local phone number. SLIP (Serial Line Internet Protocol) or PPP (Point to Point Protocol) are connections over a dial-up phone line to a service provider that allows direct connection to the Internet. Direct connection (node) is a computer with a network card wired to a local area network (LAN) or wide area network (WAN) which links directly to the Internet. When connecting via SLIP, PPP, or node, you must be running TCP/IP (Transmission Control Protocol/Internet Protocol) on your workstation. This allows data to be transferred between the two networks using the same

3

protocol or language. TCP/IP was developed as the standard because data must travel over many different operating systems. The computer workstation on your desktop is considered the client. The computer you are connected with is considered the host or server.

Universities generally have high speed telephone line connections to the Internet. Many can provide dial-up access or direct access depending on the system setup. Contact the system operator to see if there is a way to gain connection through their computer network. State networks, free-nets, and public library networks are other options. Also, commercial vendors are now offering connection to the Internet for a monthly fee.

TEXT BASED DIAL-UP CONNECTION

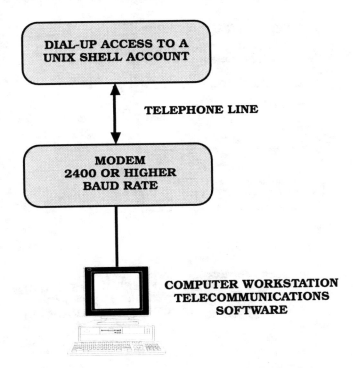

This diagram shows a standard text based dial-up connection. Universities, organizations, state governments, and some commercial vendors provide this kind of access. You dial a telephone number and are connected to a host computer. The host is running a UNIX operating system. You are asked to login with your name (userid) and a password. Once logged on, you will either see a menu screen or a system prompt (UNIX shell); sometimes both are available. A UNIX shell allows you to type in manual commands.

All you need for this dial-up connection is a computer workstation, a 2400 baud modem or higher, a standard telephone line, telecommunications software, and an account with an Internet service provider. You can gopher, FTP, telnet, e-mail, access newsgroups, and engage in chat sessions using the software at the host computer. However, you will not be able to run Mosaic or other graphical interfaces for accessing the World Wide Web.

ONLINE SERVICE CONNECTION

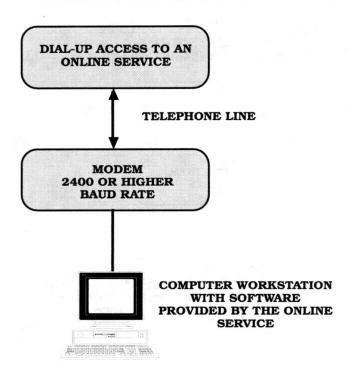

Some online services provide Internet access while allowing you to explore information provided on their own networks as well. Examples of these are America Online, CompuServe, Prodigy, and Delphi. To connect to one of these services, you need a computer workstation, 2400 baud modem or higher, standard telephone line, telecommunications software, and an account with one of these services. Many companies provide their own front end software. These graphical interfaces are user friendly and make navigating and downloading as easy as a click of the mouse button.

SLIP OR PPP CONNECTION

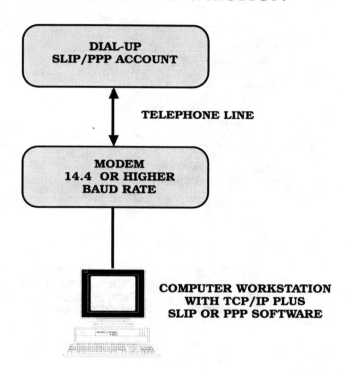

In this diagram you need a computer workstation, modem, standard telephone line, an Internet service provider that allows a SLIP (Serial Line Internet Protocol) or PPP (Point to Point Protocol) connection, and a collection of software for e-mail, FTP, gopher, and telnet. Many universities and commercial vendors provide this type of dial-up connection and software package. You must be running TCP/IP and either SLIP or PPP software. The faster the modem the better. A 9600 baud modem is adequate for running gopher, telnet, FTP, and e-mail software tools. However, if you want to run Mosaic to access the World Wide Web, you should have a 14.4 baud modem or higher.

ISDN CONNECTION

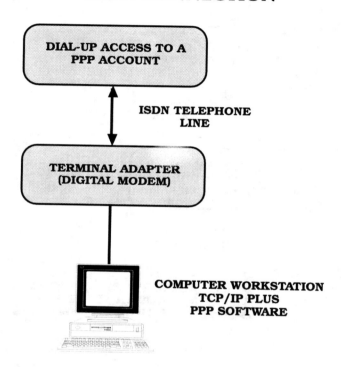

ISDN (Integrated Systems Digital Network) is a digital rather than traditional analog telephone line. It consists of two 64 kbs channels called B channels and one D or delta channel. The B channels are used for voice or data. The D channel is used for signaling or x.25 packet networking. It is not available in all areas. In order to use this setup, you must have an ISDN line installed, a computer workstation, terminal adapter, and a PPP account. You must be running TCP/IP and PPP software on your workstation. You have a full range of Internet tools, including e-mail, FTP, telnet, gopher, and newsgroups. You can also use graphical interfaces such as Mosaic for accessing the World Wide Web.

LAN OR WAN CONNECTION

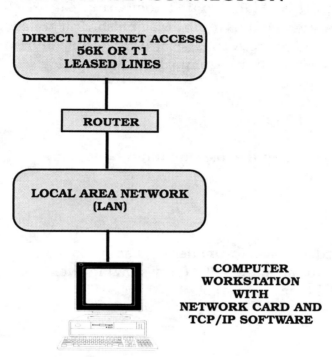

DIRECT INTERNET ACCESS
56K OR T1
LEASED LINES

ROUTER

LOCAL AREA NETWORK
(LAN)

COMPUTER
WORKSTATION
WITH
NETWORK CARD AND
TCP/IP SOFTWARE

In this option, you must be connected to a local area network (LAN) or Wide Area Network (WAN) that provides a link to the Internet via a router. You must have TCP/IP running on your workstation along with a network card. With this configuration you can run graphical user interface programs for gopher, World Wide Web, telnet, FTP, and e-mail. Files are transferred very quickly. Some video and audio capabilities are also possible with programs such as CUSeeMe (videoconferencing) and Maven (audioconferencing). You will need a workstation with at least 90Mhz processing speed and a video or digital camera. If you want to view video at 30 frames per second, you need an even faster connection such as a fiber ATM (Asynchronous Transfer Mode) and a huge amount of RAM and disk storage space.

TELECOMMUNICATIONS SOFTWARE

There are many software programs you can use to communicate with other computers. MacKermit (freeware), ZTerm (shareware), and Microphone are programs for the Macintosh. Integrated packages such as Clarisworks and Microsoft Works also contain a communications module. ProComm, Crosstalk, ProComm Plus for Windows, and Crosstalk for Windows are for use on PCs.

What You Need To Know

In order to set up the telecommunications software, you must know a few definitions.

Baud Rate

The speed at which the modem transmits data is called the baud rate. Baud rates can range from 300 (very slow) to over 14,400 (very fast). The modems sold today are usually 14,400 or 28,800 bauds.

Data Bits

Data bits are the number of ASCII characters (either 128 or 256) that the host computer will be sending. This is expressed as either 7 or 8. The standard is 8 data bits.

Parity

Parity is a form of error checking between computers. Parity settings can be even, odd, mark, space, or none. Normally error checking is not used and the parity is set to none.

Stop Bit

The stop bit marks the end of a character. The standard is 1 stop bit .

When combined, these terms are expressed as 8N1, which means 8 data bits, no parity, and 1 stop bit.

Terminal Emulation

You also need to know if terminal emulation is required by the host computer. Terminal emulation makes the host computer think it is communicating with the same kind of computer at the user site. VT100 is a common type of terminal emulation. You will need to select VT100 in the telecommunications setup if the host computer requires it.

INTERNET SOFTWARE TOOLS

When choosing a connection option (node, SLIP, PPP) that links you directly to the Internet, you need a set or suite of Internet software tools rather than a telecommunications program for your computer workstation. Once you connect via TCP/IP, SLIP, or PPP, you will run these programs to access information. You will need one for retrieving e-mail, another for gopher, and more for other functions. Commercial vendors include these Internet tools in their programs. Some examples are Internet in a Box and AIR NSF for DOS; ChameleonNFS and SuperTCP/NFS for Windows (no search tools such as gopher); and Interconn Connect II and Microphone Pro II for the Macintosh.

Many of these Internet tools are available individually as freeware or shareware from a variety of sites on the Internet or from commercial providers such as America Online or CompuServe. Some universities package a set of tools already configured for connecting to their systems, which takes the sting out of setting up connection configurations with little or no documentation.

Shareware and Freeware with anonymous FTP site:

If you are adventurous or frugal, here are some shareware (small fee to developer) and freeware (free) programs with the anonymous FTP sites for retrieving them. Many of these can also be downloaded via gopher from the Eisenhower National Clearinghouse: gopher enc.org in Internet Software Tools.

Macintosh

SLIP Manager: MacSLIP (commercial program from Trisoft)
                 1-800-531-5170

E-mail: Eudora
                 mac.archive.umich.edu in /internet/mac/email

Gopher: Turbogopher
                 mac.archive.umich.edu in /internet/mac/gopher

Telnet:	NCSA Telnet mac.archive.umich.edu in /internet/mac/telnet
FTP:	Fetch mac.archive.umich.edu in /internet/mac/ftp
Finger	Finger ftp.cyberspace.com in /pub/ppp/mac/finger
Newsreader:	NewsWatcher mac.archive.umich.edu in /internet/mac/news
WAIS	WAIS for Mac mac.archive.umich.edu in /internet/mac/wais
Optional:	CUSeeMe (videoconferencing) Be sure to read the README.FIRST file gated.cornell.edu in /pub/CU-SeeMe Maven (audioconferencing) mac.archive.umich.edu in /pub/mac/util/comm/maven1.0d23.sit.hqx

Windows

SLIP Manager:	Trumpet WinSock (shareware - $20) ftp.utas.edu.au in /pc/trumpet/wintrump
E-Mail:	PC Eudora ftp.qualcomm.com in /pceudora/windows
Gopher:	WSGopher boombox.micro.umn.edu in /pub/gopher/windows

Telnet:	Windows Socket Telnet 3270 sunsite.unc.edu in /pub/micro/pc/ms-windows/winsock/apps
	NCSA Telnet ftp.ncsa.uiuc.edu in /Telnet/DOS
FTP:	WS_FTP ftp.usma.edu in /pub/msdos/winsock.files
Finger:	WinSock Finger sunsite.unc.edu in /pub/micro/pc/ms-windows/winsock/apps
Talk:	Wintalk ftp.halcyon.com in /pub/slip/talk
Newsreader:	WinVN newstitan.ksc.nasa.gov in /pub/win3/winvn
WAIS:	Waisman ftp.cnidr.org in /pub/NIDR.tools/wais/pc/windows (must have the Winsock client software)
Package:	WinQVT/Net is a package that supplies telnet, ftp, mail, and more for Windows. biochemistry.bioc.cwru.edu in /pub/qvtnet

Optional:	CUSeeMe (videoconferencing) Be sure to read the README.FIRST file gated.cornell.edu in /pub/CU-SeeMe
	Internet VoiceChat (two-way voice conversations) archive.epas.utoronto.ca in /pub/ultrasound/submitivc11.zip

Login

Logging on to a network depends on the computer operating system at the host site. In general you will be asked for a login and a password. Your login is a form of your name. The password is either letters or a series of letters and numbers you have chosen that are unique to you and will not appear on the screen when you login. It is your security and you should consider changing it occasionally to prevent others from accessing your account. You may also be asked to select a type of terminal emulation. In most cases this is VT100.

Example:

```
ULTRIX V4.4 (Rev. 69) (bottom)
login: jdoe
Password:
Terminal type (VT100):
```

There are different system prompts depending on the host computer.

Examples of System Prompts

{ }	MAGNUS at Ohio State University running a UNIX shell
>	UNIX
$	VAX/VMS
%	UNIX/XENIX/A/AX
:	UNIX

Common UNIX Commands

man <command>	display the manual page for the command
cd <pathname>	change directory
fse	initiates the full screen text editor if available
ls	list files (list current directory)
more <file name>	display the contents of a file (space bar to continue)

mm	the Columbia MM electronic mail package
rn	the USENET news access command
cp <file1> <file2>	the UNIX copy command
mv <file1> <file2>	the UNIX move command (*rename* and/or relocate a file)
rm <file name>	the UNIX remove command (*erase* or *delete* a file)
pico	initiates the pico text editor if available
pine	initiates the pine e-mail system if available
printacs <file>	print the contents of a file (*man printacs* for more info)
logout	this is how you would normally end you UNIX session
menu	this will take you into the main menu system

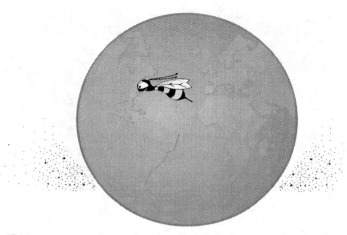

CHAPTER 2

Communicating
With Others

E-mail

Electronic mail allows you to communicate with others over a network. The advantages of e-mail are instant correspondence with colleagues, access to listserv discussion groups, and a presence in the global community.

There are whois directories or white pages for finding a person's e-mail address. Your Internet provider often will have a directory of the people with accounts on their system. Generally you can search for a person by typing in their name. Other systems provide a directory that is more globally oriented. There is no one directory listing of all the people on the Internet.

Many different types of e-mail programs allow you to communicate over the Internet. The basic information you must know is the address of the person for correspondence and a few commands. Internet addresses are expressed in terms of the userid (user identification) at the place where the person has an account called the domain or host. Here is an example of an e-mail address:

userid@domain (also called host)
jdoe@magnus.acs.ohio-state.edu

In this example, one of the subdomain extensions for the host is edu. It tells you that this is an educational institution. You can also identify the geographical location of hosts such as the United States by the extension us.

Here are some common subdomains:

com	commercial
edu	education
gov	government
int	international
mil	military
net	network
org	organization

E-mail Programs

• ELM

To send e-mail using the UNIX system or ELM type the following:

At the command prompt >	**m** [mail]
To:	**userid@domain**
Subject:	topic for discussion
Cc:	address of a person you want to receive a carbon copy or press return for none

Type your message.

Type **control-e**, then **s** to send the message.

Additional Commands

To reply to an e-mail message:

At the system prompt >   highlight the message to which you want to reply and type **r**

You are now in the area for typing your message. The mailer already has the address and subject for your reply. Use the send command for your system to send the message.

To delete a message:

At the system prompt >   highlight the message you want to delete and type **d**
In a UNIX shell type **d** and the number

Example: > **d 1** or **d 1-5**

To undelete a message:

At the system prompt >   highlight the message and type **u**
                          In a UNIX shell type **u** and the number

                          Example: > **u 1**

To save a message:

At the system prompt >   highlight the message and type **s**
                          In a UNIX shell type **s** and the filename

                          Example: > **s education**

• VMS

The VMS mail system uses a different addressing style:

At the system prompt >   **m**
To: **IN%"userid@domain"**
Subject: topic for discussion
Cc: address of a person you want to receive a
                          carbon copy or press return for none

Type your message.

Type **control-z** to send the message.

VMS *(Continued)*

Additional Commands

At the system prompt >   type **r** after reading the message

   You are now in the area for typing your message. The mailer already has the address and subject for your reply. Use **control-z** to send the message.

        To delete a message:

At the system prompt >   type **d** and the number

                                Example: > **d 1** or **d 1-5**

        To undelete a message:

At the system prompt >   type **u** and the number

                                Example: > **u 1**

        To save a message:

At the system prompt >   type **s** and the filename

                                Example: > **s education**

• PINE

The Pine e-mail system is menu driven and easy to use:

Main Menu

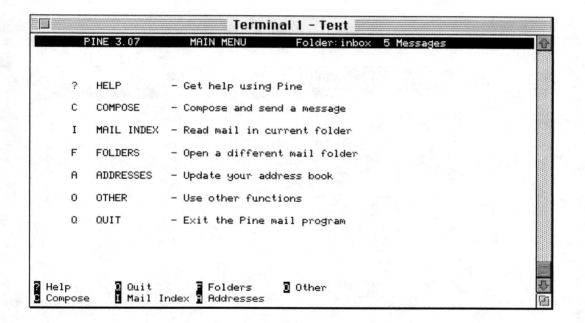

To get help, type **?**.

To compose and send a message, type **C**.

To read mail in a current folder, type **I**.

To open another folder, type **F** or **L** depending on which version of Pine is running.

To open the address menu and add e-mail addresses, type **A**.

To find other functions, type **O**. In some versions of Pine, this is listed as Setup and you would type **S**.

To quit the Pine program and go to the main menu, type **Q**.

Help Menu

```
┌──────────────────── Terminal 1 - Text ────────────────────┐
│    PINE 3.07          HELP FOR MAIN MENU        page 1 of 26  │
│                                                              │
│     HELP TEXT FOR MAIN MENU                          Page 1  │
│ Contents:     1.  Whom to Call for More Help........... 2    │
│               2.  Main Menu Commands .................  3    │
│ Frequently Asked Questions:                                  │
│               3.  Printing on PCs and Macs............ 6     │
│               4.  Stuck in Read-only mode............. 7     │
│               5.  If ^C Doesn't Work on a Mac......... 8     │
│               6.  Block deletes and paste in the composer... 9 │
│               7.  Signature files.................... 10    │
│               8.  What is MIME?...................... 11    │
│               9.  Alternate editor for composing messages.. 12 │
│              10.  Dialing in with Pine............... 13    │
│              11.  Giving Commands in Pine............ 14    │
│              12.  Notes on Pine Screens.............. 17    │
│              13.  History and Origin of Pine......... 18    │
│              14.  Pine 3.0 update ................... 23    │
│              15.  Pine contributors.................. 24    │
│              16.  Copyright notice................... 25    │
│                                                              │
│ ▌ Main Menu  ▤ Exit Help          ▐ Prev Page               │
│              ▐ Print    SPACE Next Page        ▌ Where is    │
└──────────────────────────────────────────────────────────────┘
```

To return to the Main Menu, type **M**.

To exit the help menu, type **E**.

To print the current text, type **L** or **Y** depending on which version of Pine is running.

To go to the next page, press the **space bar**.

To go back a page, press the **-** key.

To locate text, type **W** then type in the word or words you want to find.

Compose Message Menu 1

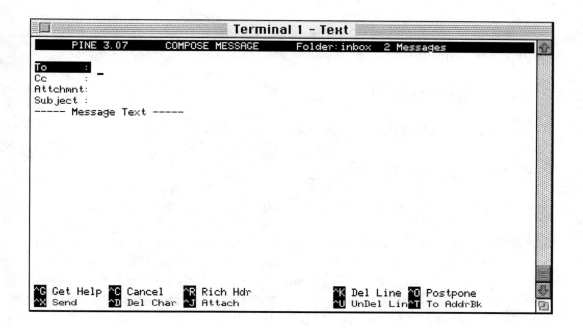

Sending an E-mail Message

From the Main Menu, type **c** (do not press the enter or return key).

To:	**userid@domain**
Cc:	address of a person you want to receive a carbon copy or press return for none
Attchmnt:	filename to send with the e-mail message
Subject:	topic for discussion

Type your message.

Type **control-x** to send the message.

Additional Commands

To get help, type **control-G**.

To cancel a message, type **control-C**.

To delete one letter, type **control-D**.

To add a blind carbon copy (Bcc:) and a file carbon copy (Fcc:), type **R**.

To attach a file that is located on your workstation, type **control-J**. When you initiate the send mail command (**control-X**), you will be asked for the transfer protocol. Start the upload command in your telecommunications software program. Point to the file you want to attach to your mail and the file will be transferred from your workstation.

To delete an entire line, type **control-K**.

To undelete, type **control-U**.

To postpone your mail, type **control-O**.

To automatically add an address from your address book, place the cursor in either the To: or From: fields, then type **control-T**.

Compose Message Menu 2

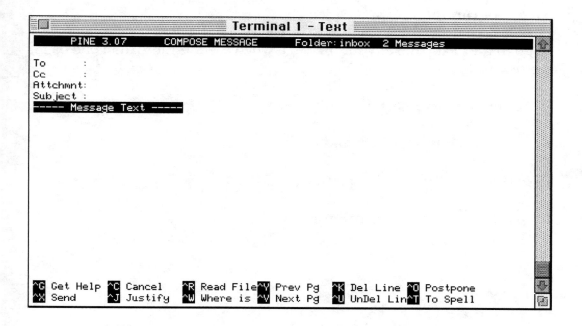

When you type your message, you have access to these commands:

To get help, type **control-G**.

To send an e-mail message, type **control-X**.

To cancel a message and return to the Main Menu, type **control-C**.

To add a common length to each line, type **control-J**.

To insert a text file into the message, type **control-R**. (This command may not work on all systems).

To search for text in the message, type **control-W**.

To go to the previous page of your message when there is more than one page, type **control-Y**.

To go to the next page of your message when there is more than one page, type **control-V**.

To delete an entire line, type **control-K**.

To undelete a line, type **control-U**.

To postpone the message, type **control-O**.

To start a spell check, type **control-T**.

Mail Index (Inbox) Menu 1

You can use your up and down arrow keys to move between messages.

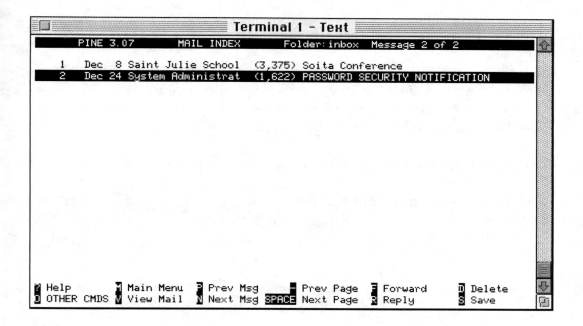

To get help, type **?**.

To access other commands, type **O**.

To go back to the Main Menu, type **M**.

To view your message, highlight the message and type **V** or the return key.

To go to a previous message, type **P**.

To go to the next message, type **N**.

To go back a page, press the - key.

To go to the next page, press the **space bar**.

To forward a message, highlight the message and type **F**. Then type the address.

To reply to a message, highlight the message and type **R**. You can choose whether or not to include the original message in your reply. You will then be in the compose screen to type your reply.

To delete a message, highlight the message and type **D**.

To save a message, highlight the message and type **S**. Then type the name of the folder in which you want to save your message. You can type the name of an existing folder, create a new name, or use the default, which is **saved-messages**.

Mail Index (Inbox) Menu 2

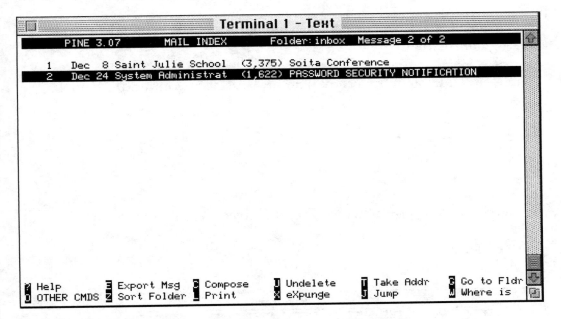

To get help, type **?**.

To go to other commands, type **O**.

To transfer a message to your workstation, type **E**. Then give the file a name and choose a protocol for downloading.

To sort the order in which your messages appear on the screen, type **Z**. You can choose from the following: by subject, arrival time, sender, date, size, and reverse arrival time.

To go to the compose menu, type **C**.

To print a message, type **L** or **Y** depending on which version of Pine is running.

31

To undelete a message, type **U**.

To expunge a message with a D next to it, type **X**. This will delete the message immediately.

To take an address in the From: field and add it to your address book, type **T**.

To go to a message, type **J**.

To go to a folder, type **G**.

To search message headers (To:, From:, Subject:, etc.), type **W**.

Folder Menu

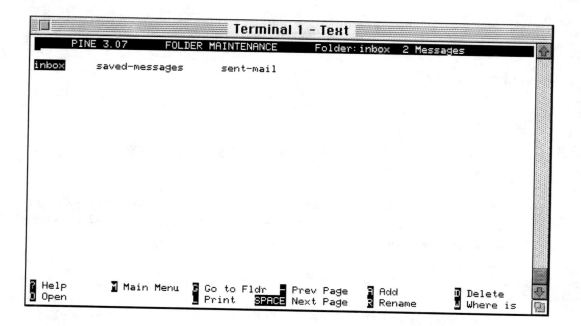

At the main menu type **F** or **L** to go to the folders menu. Your messages are stored in folders. The inbox contains all of your incoming mail. The save-messages folder holds mail that you want to save. The sent-messages folder contains copies of the messages you have mailed to others.

To get help, type **?**.

To open the folder and look at the messages, type **O**.

To go back to Pine's Main Menu, type **M**.

To go to any folder, type **G**. You will be asked which folder to open.

To print the list of folders, type **L** or **Y** depending on which version of Pine is running.

If you have more than one page of folders, type **-** to go up a page or press the **space bar** to go down a page.

To create a new folder, type **A** . Then type the new folder name.

To rename a folder, highlight it (use the arrow keys to highlight) and type **R**, then the new name.

To delete an entire folder and all of its contents, highlight it, then type **D**.

To search for a folder by name, type **W**.

Downloading Mail Files

(This may not be available on all systems).

1. Save the message to a folder such as saved-messages.

2. From the Main Menu, type **F** to open the Folder Menu.

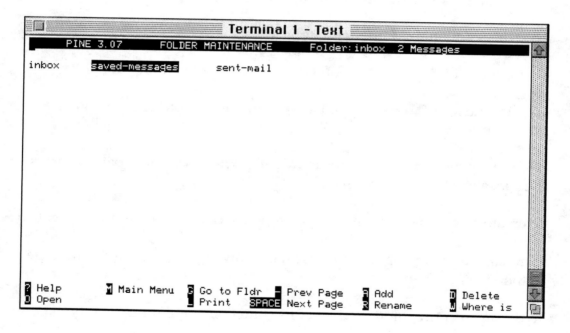

3. To download the contents of the saved-messages folder, highlight the folder by using the tab key.

4. Type **s**.

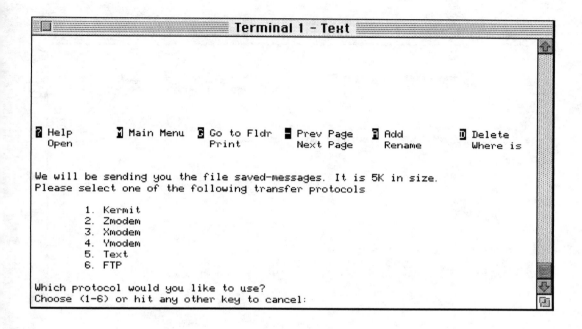

```
╔════════════════════ Terminal 1 - Text ════════════════════╗
║                                                          ▲║
║                                                           ║
║                                                           ║
║                                                           ║
║                                                           ║
║                                                           ║
║ ▓ Help      ▓ Main Menu  ▓ Go to Fldr ▓ Prev Page ▓ Add      ▓ Delete ║
║   Open                     Print         Next Page   Rename    Where is║
║                                                           ║
║ We will be sending you the file saved-messages. It is 5K in size.║
║ Please select one of the following transfer protocols     ║
║                                                           ║
║         1. Kermit                                         ║
║         2. Zmodem                                         ║
║         3. Xmodem                                         ║
║         4. Ymodem                                         ║
║         5. Text                                           ║
║         6. FTP                                            ║
║                                                          ▓║
║ Which protocol would you like to use?                    ▼║
║ Choose (1-6) or hit any other key to cancel:             ▣║
╚═══════════════════════════════════════════════════════════╝
```

5. You will be asked to choose a transfer protocol. Choose a protocol that
   your telecommunications software supports.

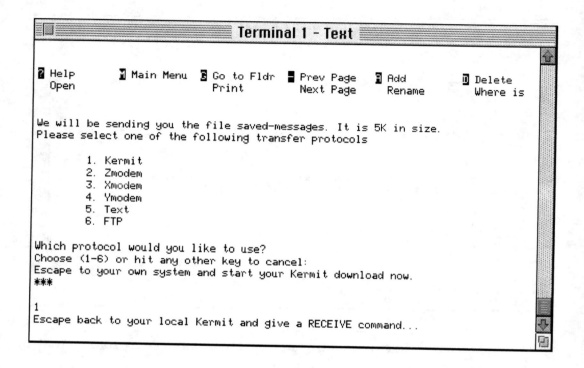

```
▣ Help        ▣ Main Menu  ▣ Go to Fldr  ▣ Prev Page  ▣ Add     ▣ Delete
  Open                        Print        Next Page    Rename    Where is


We will be sending you the file saved-messages. It is 5K in size.
Please select one of the following transfer protocols

        1. Kermit
        2. Zmodem
        3. Xmodem
        4. Ymodem
        5. Text
        6. FTP

Which protocol would you like to use?
Choose (1-6) or hit any other key to cancel:
Escape to your own system and start your Kermit download now.
***

1
Escape back to your local Kermit and give a RECEIVE command...
```

6. Execute the receive command in your telecommunications program and the file will be transferred to your workstation.

Address Book

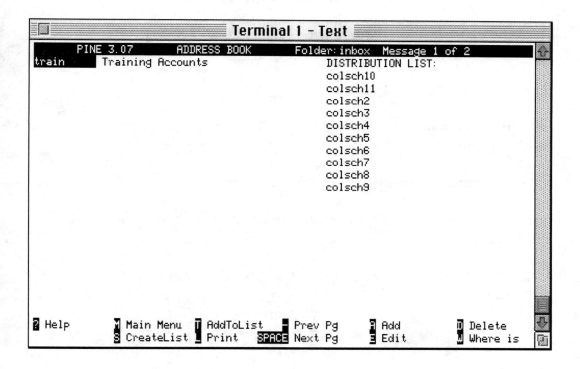

In the address book, you can create an "alias" to denote a person's e-mail address:

1. Type **a** to add a person's e-mail address.

2. At the **New Full Name: last, first** prompt, type in the new person's full name (Names are automatically alphabetized).

3. At the **new nickname:** prompt, type in the new nickname.

4. At the **e-mail address:** prompt, type in the person's e-mail address.

In the previous sample screen, the word train is the alias for Training Accounts. This is also an example of a distribution list.

To create a distribution list where one message will go to everyone on the list, follow these steps:

1. Type **S** to create a distribution list.

2. At the **Long name/description of new list:** prompt, type the name and list description.

3. At the **list nickname:** prompt, type in the nickname.

4. At the **1st address or blank when done:** prompt, type in the address of the first person on your list.

5. Continue until you have entered all of the addresses you want in your distribution list.

Other Menu

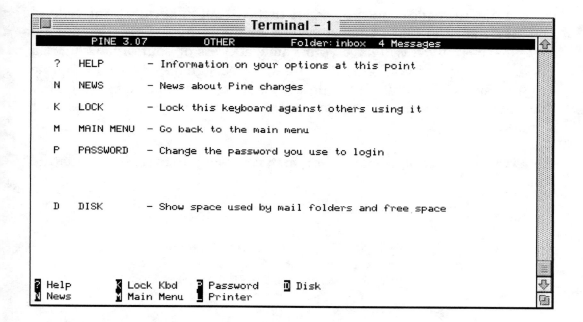

To get help, type **?**.

To get an update about the Pine program, type **N**.

To keep others from using you keyboard, type **K** to lock it. You will need your password to unlock it.

To go to the Main Menu, type **M**.

To change your online password, type **P**.

To change the printer default, type **L**. Check with your system operator for the proper setting. If you have a dial-up connection, the setting is probably attached-to-ANSI.

To check your disk usage (how much storage space your files are occupying on the system), type **D**.

Signature File

The signature file is one you create that will automatically be appended to your e-mail and Usenet messages. Your signature is information unique to you. Generally, it will have your name, address of your organization, a phone number, and your e-mail address. Some signatures contain a quote or witticism. The established netiquette is that the signature be no longer than four lines. Some systems have a menu area where you can create your signature file.

Here is an example of a menu program that allows you to create a signature file:

```
E-Mail Signature

    By default, the e-mails you send do not have a signature
    automatically added at the end.  You may choose to create
    such a signature and have it be added to all e-mails you
    send.

    Signatures should be no longer than 75 characters per line
    and can be no more than 4 lines long.

    Your current signature is:



    Selection choices:
            press E to edit your signature
            press R to remove your signature
            press any other key to go back to the Free-Net

Enter your choice:
```

If your system does not have this menu area, you may create a signature manually. Here's how to do it:

Step 1. At the system prompt, start a text editor such as pico.   > **pico**
Step 2. Enter the signature information you want attached to your e-mail.
Step 3. Save the file as **.signature**.

To Create a Signature with ELM:

In order to have ELM attach a signature file, you must edit the elmrc file.

Step 1. Change your directory to the one containing **elmrc** file. This is probably your Mail or .elm directory.

Step 2.   At the system prompt start a screen editor such as fse.
> **fse elmrc**

Step 3. Move the cursor to the line below:

local ".signature" file to append to appropriate messages...

Press control-f to move down a page at a time

At remotesignature = type the name of your signature file. The two lines should now read:

#local ".signature" file to append to appropriate messages...
localsignature = <signature filename>

Step 4. Continue moving the cursor to the line below:

#remote ".signature file to append to appropriate messages...

At the remotesignature = type the name of your signature file. The two lines should now read:

#remote ".signature file to append to appropriate messages...
remote signature = <signature filename>

Example of a signature file:

```
Jane C. Doe                        Somewhere Public Schools
Library Media Specialist           Main Street
xxx-xxx-xxxx                       Anytown, Ohio 43211
jdoe@magnus.acs.ohio-state.edu
```

A Word About Smiles or Smileys

When communicating on the Internet, your facial expressions and vocal intonations are not visible or audible. You might say something you think is funny, but the person on the receiving end may not understand. This is where smiles come into play. Smiles are typed character patterns on the screen that help the reader understand the meaning of what you are saying. There are some basic designs as well as more elaborate ones and they are fun to create. In fact, there are smile dictionaries available on the Internet. The *Unofficial Smile Dictionary* by Guy Kawasaki is one example.

Here are the basics taken from the Unofficial Smile Dictionary:

The Unofficial Smilie Dictionary

:-)   Your basic smilie. This smilie is used to inflect a sarcastic or joking statement since we can't hear voice inflection over Unix.

;-)   Winky smilie. User just made a flirtatious and/or sarcastic remark. More of a "don't hit me for what I just said" smilie.

:-(Frowning smilie. User did not like that last statement or is upset or depressed about something.

:-I   Indifferent smilie. Better than a Frowning smilie but not quite as good as a happy smilie

:->   User just made a really biting sarcastic remark. Worse than a :-).

>:->   User just made a really devilish remark.

>;->   Winky and devil combined. A very lewd remark was just made.

For those of you who love the "Mouse," here are two from the Disney News Group:

```
()~()
(_)  Minnie Mouse
```

```
()_()
(_)  Mickey Mouse
```

Cow lovers, check this one out!

```
    A/~~\A     'moo2u from osu'
   ((0   0))_____
     \  /    the  \
    (-)\   OSU   |
```

LISTSERVS

A listserv is a discussion group interested in a specific topic. In order to participate in the discussion group, you must subscribe to the listserv group. Subscription is free. Subscribing simply means you sign up to receive the messages via e-mail. Hundreds of people subscribe to these groups and the messages can accumulate quickly. You will need to read your mail frequently to keep up with the postings. To find listservs targeted to the education community, read *An Educator's Guide to E-Mail Lists* by Prescott Smith, *Directory of Scholarly Conferences* by Diane Kovacs, or *IRD Vol. 2 Listservs* by Judi Harris available from the University of Michigan Clearinghouse.

URL: gopher://una.hh.lib.umich.edu:70/11/inetdirsstacks

gopher gopher.lib.umich.edu

Gopher Path:

World Wide Gophers/North America/USA/Michigan/University of Michigan Libraries/ What's New and Featured/Clearinghouse/ All Guides

LISTSERV SUBSCRIPTION STEP-BY-STEP INSTRUCTIONS:

Step 1. Within your e-mail program, type **m** to initiate e-mail
Step 2. To: **listserv@host**
Step 3. Subject: leave blank
Step 5. Cc: leave blank
Step 6. In the body of the message type: **subscribe listname your name**
Step 7. End mail and send message

ELM: control-e and send
VMS: control-z
Pine: control-x

Example:

ELM:

> **m**
> To: **listserv@listserv.syr.edu**
> Subject:
> Cc:
Body of Message: **subscribe lm_net Jane Doe**
control-e, then **s** to send.

VMS:

> **MAIL**
> **m**
> To: **IN%"listserv@listserv.syr.edu"**
> Subject:
> Cc:
Body of Message: **subscribe lm_net Jane Doe**
control-z

Pine:

> **c**
> To: **listserv@listserv.syr.edu**
> Subject:
> Attchmnt:
> Cc:
Body of Message: **subscribe lm_net Jane Doe**
control-x

To leave a discussion group replace subscribe with signoff or unsubscribe depending on the listserv instructions. You receive these instructions after subscribing. Save them for future reference.

Once you are a subscriber, you will want to post messages for others in the discussion group to read. To post a message that will go to all subscribers, send mail to the discussion group address, not the listserv.

Example:
> **m**
> To: **lm_net@listserv.syr.edu**
> Subject: (this can be the subject of the message you are sending)
> Cc:
Type your message
End the mail program and send

To reply to a message that all subscribers will read simply type **r**, then type your message.

To reply to an individual, look for their Internet address in the message and send e-mail directly to them.

Sample of Educational Listservs

BigSix   Information access skills discussion group

To subscribe to the list, address an e-mail message to:
listserv@listserv.syr.edu
No subject
In the body of the message type:
subscribe BigSix your name

BR_Match   For K-12 students and teachers who would like to connect with other classrooms and choose a book to read for discussion

To subscribe to list, address an e-mail message to:
mailserv@wcu.edu

No subject
In the body of the message type:
subscribe BR_Match your name

CUSEEME   For educators interested in videoconferencing

To subscribe to the list, address an e-mail message to:
lists@gsn.org
No subject
In the body of the message type:
subscribe cu-seeme-schools your e-mail address

ECENET-L   Early childhood education (0-8 yrs).

To subscribe to the list, address an e-mail message to:
listserv@vmd.cso.uiuc.edu
No subject
In the body of the message type:
subscribe ECENET-L your name

EDNET   A forum exploring the educational potential of the Internet

To subscribe to the list, address an e-mail message to:
listserv@nic.umass.edu
No subject
In the body of the message type:
subscribe Ednet your name

EDPOLYAN   Education Policy Analysis Forum

To subscribe to the list, address an e-mail message to:
listserv@asuvm.inre.asu.edu
No subject
In the body of the message type:

subscribe EDPOLYAN your name

EDTECH   Educational technology

To subscribe to the list, address an e-mail message to:
listserv@msu.edu
No subject
In the body of the message type:
sub edtech your name

FIELDTRIPS-L For teachers who want to exchange information
about their field trips and excursions

To subscribe to the list, address an e-mail message to:
majordomo@acme.fred.org
No subject
In the body of the message type:
subscribe fieldtrips-L

IECC   For teachers who want to find partner classrooms for
international and cross-cultural electronic mail
exchange (not for individual pen pals or for discussion)

To subscribe to the list, address an e-mail message to:
iecc-request@stolaf.edu
No subject
In the body of the message type:
subscribe IECC your name

K12ADMIN   K-12 School Administrator Discussion

To subscribe to the list, address an e-mail message to:
listserv@listserv.syr.edu
No subject

In the body of the message type:
subscribe K12ADMIN your name

KIDCAFE   For kids (10 - 15) who want to communicate with other
                kids around the world

                To subscribe to the list, address an e-mail message to:
                listserv@vm1.nodak.edu
                No subject
                In the body of the message type:
                subscribe KIDCAFE your name

KIDLIT-L   For educators, librarians, researchers, authors, and others
                interested in literature for children and youths.

                To subscribe to the list address an e-mail message to:
                listserv@bingvmb.cc.binghamton.edu
                No subject
                In the body of the message type:
                subscribe KIDLIT-L your name

KIDSPHERE   To develop an international network for children &
                teachers

                To subscribe to the list, address an e-mail message to:
                kidsphere@vms.cis.pitt.edu
                No subject
                In the body of the message type:
                subscribe kidsphere your name

LM_NET   School Library Media

                To subscribe to the list, address an e-mail message to:
                listserv@listserv.syr.edu
                No subject

In the body of the message type:
subscribe LM_NET your name

MIDDLE-L   Middle School

To subscribe to the list, address an e-mail message to:
listserv@listserv.syr.edu
No subject
In the body of the message type:
subscribe middle-l your name

SOCSTUD-L   For K-12 Social Studies teachers

To subscribe to the list, address an e-mail message to:
mailserv@hcca.ohio.gov
No subject
In the body of the message type:
subscribe SOCSTUD-L your name

SUPERK12   School networking and telecommunications

To subscribe to the list, address an e-mail message to:
listserv@listserv.syr.edu
No subject
In the body of the message type:
subscribe SUPERK12 your name

VOCNET   Vocational Education Practitioners

To subscribe to the list, address an e-mail message to:
listserv@cmsa.berkeley.edu
No subject
In the body of the message type:
Subscribe VOCNET your name

Newsgroups

Networks provide literally thousands of discussion groups that can be read using a newsreader. The newsgroups are organized into seven Usenet groups: comp, news, rec, sci, soc, talk, and misc. There are other newsgroups that are similar to Usenet, but have different names. These are alt, bionet, bit, biz, de, fi, ieee, gnu, k12, u3b, and vmsnet. There is also Clarinet, which is an indexed system of United Press International (UPI) and syndicated columns. This service is limited to organizations that contract for the service. There are several UNIX newsreader programs to choose from: rn, nn, trn, and tin. Consult your system administrator to see which one is available to you.

K12NET NEWSGROUPS

Conference Areas Available in K12Net

=====================================

Contact your sysop if ALL of these conferences are not available locally as per K12Net policy.

USENET Newsgroup	FidoNet Echo	Description
k12.lang.francais	K12_FRANCAIS	French Conversation
k12.lang.esp-eng	K12_SPAN_ENG	Spanish Conversation
k12.lang.deutsch-eng	K12_GERM_ENG	German Conversation
k12.lang.russian	K12_RUSSIAN	Russian Conversation
k12.lang.art	K12_LANG_ART	Language Arts Education
k12.ed.tag	K12_TAG	Talented and Gifted
k12.ed.art	K12_ART_ED	Art Education
k12.ed.music	K12_MUSIC_ED	Music Education
k12.ed.business	K12_BUS_ED	Business Education
k12.ed.health-pe	K12_HLTH_PE	Health & Physical Education
k12.ed.life-skills	K12_LIF_SKIL	School Counselors
k12.ed.soc-studies	K12_SOC_STUD	Social Studies Education
k12.ed.tech	K12_TECH_ED	Technical/Vocational Education

k12.ed.science	K12_SCI_ED	Science Education
k12.ed.math	K12_MATH_ED	Math Education
k12.ed.comp.literacy	K12_COMP_LIT	Computer Literacy
k12.ed.special	K12_SPEC_ED	Special Education
k12.chat.teacher	K12.TCH_CHAT	Teacher Chat
k12.library	LIBRARY	Technology in Libraries

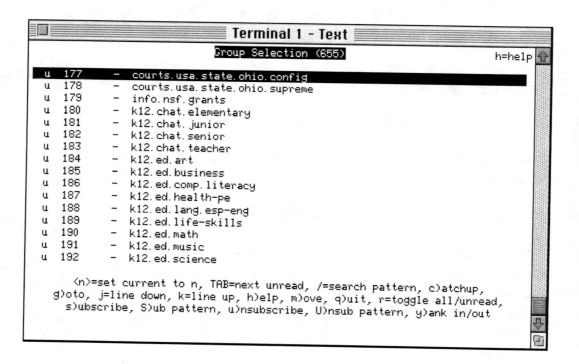

```
                    Terminal 1 - Text
                 Group Selection (655)                        h=help

 u  177    -   courts.usa.state.ohio.config
 u  178    -   courts.usa.state.ohio.supreme
 u  179    -   info.nsf.grants
 u  180    -   k12.chat.elementary
 u  181    -   k12.chat.junior
 u  182    -   k12.chat.senior
 u  183    -   k12.chat.teacher
 u  184    -   k12.ed.art
 u  185    -   k12.ed.business
 u  186    -   k12.ed.comp.literacy
 u  187    -   k12.ed.health-pe
 u  188    -   k12.ed.lang.esp-eng
 u  189    -   k12.ed.life-skills
 u  190    -   k12.ed.math
 u  191    -   k12.ed.music
 u  192    -   k12.ed.science

    <n>=set current to n, TAB=next unread, /=search pattern, c)atchup,
  g)oto, j=line down, k=line up, h)elp, m)ove, q)uit, r=toggle all/unread,
   s)ubscribe, S)ub pattern, u)nsubscribe, U)nsub pattern, y)ank in/out
```

This is an example of the tin newsreader with the commands listed at the bottom of the screen.

MUDS

Enter the world of virtual reality on the Internet. MUDS are multi-user domains or programs where you take on a character, go exploring, encounter others, and solve puzzles. It is similar to Dungeons and Dragons. To reach a MUD, you can telnet or use a client program. The following two MOOs (multi-user object oriented mud) are designed for K-12 education.

StarkNet

URL: telnet://bigbird.stark.k12.oh.us@guest:7777

telnet bigbird.stark.k12.oh.us 7777 login: guest

```
oooooooooo.      .oooooo.    ooooo       ooo ooooo      ooo oooooooooooo
'888'     'Y8b   d8P'  'Y8b  '888b.      '8' '888'      '8' 8'   888    '8
 888      888 888       888  8 '88b.     8   888        8        888
 888      888 888       888  8  '88b.    8   888        8        888
 888      888 888       888  8   '88b.8  888        8        888
 888     d88' '88b     d88'  8    '888  '88.   .8'       888
o888bood8P'  'Y8bood8P'  o8o        '8   'YbodP'         o888o
         (eDucational mOo: starkNet campUs of the fuTure)

              StarkNet School of the Future
_ _ _ _ _ _ _ _ _ _ _ _ _ _ _ _ _ _ _ _ _ _ _ _ _ _ _ _ _ _ _ _
'COnnect <character-name> <password>' to connect as a registered
user,
'COnnect guest' to connect as a guest here on DONUT,
'@who' or 'Who' to see who's logged in right now, or,
'@quit'      to disconnect, either now or later.
_ _ _ _ _ _ _ _ _ _ _ _ _ _ _ _ _ _ _ _ _ _ _ _ _ _ _ _ _ _ _ _

About DONUT Moo.

Welcome to DONUT Moo, StarkNet's Multi-User, Object-Oriented, Virtual
Reality. Students from all over Stark County, Ohio, have collaborated
to build the Virtual School of the Future, and are busy designing
interdisciplinary educational exhibits, in a constructionist
environment.
```

Come and visit us. Just type "connect Guest," when you see the Welcome Screen. If you are new to MOOs, just type HELP to get started, after you have connected. To disconnect when you are finished, type @quit. See you there!

FredNet MOO

URL: http://fred.net/cindy/moo.html

telnet fred.net 8888 login: connect guest

```
*******  FredNet MOO Grand Opening Celebration  Feb 18-20  *******
-=-=-=-=-=-=-=-=-=-=-=-=-=-=-=-=-=-=-=-=-=-=-=-=-=-=-=-=-=-=-=-=-=
```

Once on the MOO, type HELP @REQUEST for instructions on how to get an account.

Some callers here are working; some are relaxing. Every visitor is expected to behave politely and respect the rights of others.

*** Connected ***

Visitor Center

```
    /~~[F]ictional~~~~[M]OO Towns:~~~~~~~[LIB]rary:  (Help Room)
   /      Worlds        small & large           \ (Generics)
  /                                              \(Tutorials)
 /                                                \

 @QUIT                                     [C]onvention
 <-               Visitor Center            Center ->
                                                      __
 \                                               /
  \                                             /
   \                                           /
    \___[R]esidential_____[S]chool District____/
```

You see Graffiti Wall, Directory, World Clock, Credits, and Notepad here.

FINGER

The finger command gives you information about a person . It will tell you their account name and location as well as the last time they logged on to the system. In addition, a .plan file can be created by the individual that is readable worldwide. The information provided in this .plan file can range from conference dates to the latest earthquake information. For example, suppose you were conducting a workshop about educational reform. You could post the syllabus in your finger file for others to view.

At the system prompt > **finger userid@host**

    Example: > **finger jdoe@magnus.acs.ohio-state.edu**

You would receive this information about the person and see that the .plan file is a happy greeting:

```
Login: jdoe                     Name: Jane C. Doe
Directory: /acs/bottom/2/jdoe     Shell: /usr/local/bin/tcsh
On beauty since Sun Jun 12 15:57 (EDT) on ttypb from sonngate-9600.acs.ohio-
stat
e.edu
Last login Sun Jun 12 15:57 (EDT)
Plan:
"May the sun shine upon your rooftop
 And the rain bounce up against your barefeet"
```

Here is an example where an individual has posted timely events and a sports schedule as their .plan file and deleted personal information.

    Example: > **finger copi@oddjob.uchicago.edu**

You would receive this information:

```
                      Saturday
                    June  4, 1994
                   6:38:12 PM (CDT)

           Greenwich Mean Time: 11:38:12 PM

         Day 155 and Week 22 of current year
         13,372,692 seconds elapsed in current year
         204 shopping days until Christmas

           Phase of moon: waning crescent
         Age of moon 4 days (to next new moon)

                 The year of the Dog

         ***************** Special Events ******************
         * Birth: King George III (England) (256 years ago) *
         * Death: Ayatollah Ruhollah Khomeini (5 years ago) *
         **************** Event: Donut Day ****************
         **** Event: 1st minimum wage law (82 years ago) ****
         * Event: Massacre in Tianamen Square (5 years ago) *
         ****************************************************
```

```
Here is a list of upcoming games
  (note: all times are EDT)
MLB schedule for today...
    (WGN)   White Sox    at Orioles      (7:05 pm)
            Indians      at Athletics    (4:05 pm)
            Royals       at Yankees      (1:35 pm)
   (WTBS)   Dodgers      at Braves       (7:10 pm)
            Brewers      at Angels       (10:05 pm)
            Twins        at Tigers       (1:15 pm)
    (WGN)   Expos        at Cubs         (2:20 pm)
            Mets         at Reds         (7:05 pm)
            Phillies     at Astros       (8:05 pm)
            Pirates      at Rockies      (9:05 pm)
            Padres       at Marlins      (7:05 pm)
            Giants       at Cardinals    (8:05 pm)
            Rangers      at Red Sox      (1:05 pm)
```

56

Creating a .plan File:

Step 1. Be sure you are in the system shell.

Step 2. At the system prompt > start a text editor such as pico or fse.
Start your editor by typing the word **pico** or **fse**.

Step 3. Type what you want for your .plan (you might want to leave a blank line at the top to separate it from the rest of your finger information).

Step 4. When finished typing your file, exit your editor.
In pico it is **control-x**   In fse it is **control-e**

Step 5. save: **y**

Step 6. file: **.plan** (You must name the file .plan)
Hint: When you list the files in your directory .plan will not be listed. It is an invisible file. However, you can still read it and edit it. To read it, type **more .plan**. To edit the file, start your text editor. When your text editor asks for which file to insert, type .plan

Step 7. At the system prompt, type **chmod a+r ~/.plan** (makes the file world readable). The chmod command changes the access mode of one or more files.

Step 8. At the system prompt, type **chmod a+x ~** (makes the file world executable).

Step 9. At the system prompt, type **ls -ld ~** (to check the file).
It should look like this:
drwx—x—x
Another way to check is to finger your own address. You should see what you typed in your .plan file

T ALK

Two-way conversations can take place on Internet using the UNIX talk program. You do not actually communicate by speaking, but by typing messages back and forth on a split screen. Both parties can agree to communicate at a specified time if they are in different locations. If both have accounts at the same host, either can check to see if the other person is logged on and initiate a talk session.

To initiate a talk session:

At the system prompt > type **talk** and the person's **userid@host**

Example: > **talk jdoe@ohionet.org**

A message will appear on their screen:

Message from Talk_Daemon@ohionet.org at 10:03
talk: connection requested by user@magnus.acs.ohio-state.edu
talk: respond with: talk user@magnus.acs.ohio-state.edu

To respond to the talk request:

At the system prompt > type **talk user@host**

Example: > **talk user @magnus.acs.ohio-state.edu**

To break the connection press **control-c**.

CHAPTER 3

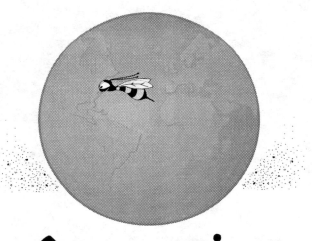

Accessing Information

GOPHER

gopher n. 1. Any of various short tailed, burrowing mammals of
the family Geomyidae, of North America. 2. (Amer. colloq.)
Native or inhabitant of Minnesota: the Gopher State.
3. (Amer. colloq.) One who runs errands, does odd-jobs, fetches
or delivers documents for office staff. 4. (computer tech.)
Software following a simple protocol for tunneling through a TCP/
IP internet.

The gopher system, developed by the University of Minnesota, is one of
the best ways to begin exploration. Gopher is an easy-to-use menu-driven
system that you can utilize to access information from many different Internet
sites all over the world simply by "pointing" and going to them. This is
called traveling through gopherspace. You will need to check with your
system administrator at your school to see if your Internet connection
provides access to its own gopher system. If not, you can reach a gopher
system by typing gopher followed by a gopher "address."

At the system prompt > type gopher and the internet address

Example: **gopher nwoca7.nwoca.ohio.gov**

Once you reach the main menu, you can choose from a list of subjects.
You simply type the number or "point" the arrow key at the site you want
to go to and then press the return key. Another menu appears with more
choices. At the bottom of the screen is a list of commands for navigating
through the menus. By continuing to make selections, you are burrowing
deeper into the gopher hole. See the following examples.

NWOCA/OECCN K-12 Student Gopher Server

1. About the OECN Gopher Server
2. How to Obtain Changes to This Gopher Server
3. Outline of This Gopher Server
4. Government Center
5. Library Center
6. Local Time and Temperature (Toledo, Ohio USA)
7. NW Ohio Alliance of Professional Development Providers (NWOAPDP)
8. NWOCA Electronic Mail Address Listing
9. Ohio Department of Education (ODE) Resources
10. Other Information Resources
--> 11. Reference Center
12. School House
13. Weather Center

Reference Center

-->1. Acronym Dictionary Search
2. American English Dictionary (Searchable)
3. Best Market Reports (UMich)
4. CIA World Factbook 1993 (Searchable) at NWOCA
5. CIA World Factbook 1994 (Searchable) at NWOCA
6. County Codes Used for Network Domains
7. County Codes of the World [ISO 3166]
8. Currency Exchange Rates (UN)
9. Elementary & Fundamental Particles of Matter
10. Geographic Name Server
11. Geologic Progression Timetable
12. German/English Dictionary (UToledo)
13. International System of Units
14. Mathematical Values
15. Monetary Statistics
16. Periodic Table of the Elements (rev. 3/93)
17. Roget's Thesaurus (Published 1911)
18. Roget's Thesaurus Search (from Brown Univ.)

Moving Around Gopherspace

Press return to view a document

Use the Arrow Keys or vi/emacs equivalent to move around

Up ....: Move to previous line.
Down ....: Move to next line.
Right Return ....: "Enter"/Display current item.
Left, u ....: "Exit" current item/Go up a level.

>, +, Pgdwn, space ..: View next page.
<, -, Pgup, b ....: View previous page.

0-9 ....: Go to a specific line.
m ....: Go back to the main menu.

Bookmarks

a :   Add current item to the bookmark list.
A :   Add current directory/search to bookmark list.
v :   View bookmark list.
d :   Delete a bookmark/directory entry.

Other commands

s :   Save current item to a file.
D :   Download a file.
q :   Quit with prompt.
Q :   Quit unconditionally.
= :   Display Technical information about current item.
O :   change options
/ :   Search for an item in the menu.
n :   Find next search item.
o :   Open a new gopher server
! :   Shell Escape

Exploring Gopherspace

Gopherspace is an ever changing environment. What you see today may not be there tomorrow. New sites come up daily; others disappear. Some servers move to new "addresses." If you don't know the address or location for information, how do you find it? How do you remember sites you have already found? There are some programs designed to work with gopher that will make your life a little bit easier.

Veronica and Jughead

Veronica and Jughead are programs that allow you to search for information in gopherspace by keyword. Veronica searches all of gopherspace, while Jughead searches a specific gopher server at one location. Veronica and Jughead can be accessed through the gopher system. Look for them on one of the gopher menu screens. For example, point the arrow key at the entry for searching gopherspace on one of the gopher servers you are using and type the word "earthquake." Veronica searches all gopherspace — all gophers on the Internet — searching for that character string in the menu title. After executing the search, Veronica will return a list of items matching that keyword, or more precisely that character string. To reach an item on the list, point to it and press return. You are off again, gophering to that site.

VERONICA AND JUGHEAD STEP-BY-STEP INSTRUCTIONS:

Step 1. Connect to an Internet Gopher Server.
Step 2. Select a Menu Item such as Search Gopherspace using Veronica or Search Site using Jughead.
Step 4. Select either a Jughead or a Veronica site.
Step 5. Type the keyword.
Step 6. Receive results.

Veronica servers generally search only the first 200 items. You can have Veronica search more than this number by typing **-m** after the keyword in the search box. Here's an example:

> **earthquake -m500** will provide 500 items
> **earthquake -m** will provide all available matching items

Use **-m** when you see a message such as this at the end of your search:
***234 more items matching your query

Example of Veronica Search:

```
                Search title in Gopherspace using Veronica

    1.  FAQ:  Frequently-Asked Questions about veronica  (1993-..      <Text
                                                                        File>
    2.                                                              <Text File>
    3.  Search gopherspace (veronica) via University of Koeln    <Word Search>
    4.  Search gopherspace (veronica) via U.Texas, Dallas        <Word Search>
    5.  Search gopherspace (veronica) via University of Pisa     <Word Search>
 -> 6.  Search gopherspace (veronica) via NYSERNet               <Word Search>
    7.  Search gopherspace (veronica) via UNINETT..U. of Bergen  <Word Search>
    8.  Search gopherspace (veronica) via SCS Nevada             <Word Search>
    9.  Search Gopher Directory Titles via University of Koel..  <Word Search>
   10.  Search Gopher Directory Titles via U.Texas, Dallas       <Word Search>
   11.  Search Gopher Directory Titles via University of Pisa    <Word Search>
   12.  Search Gopher Directory Titles via NYSERNet              <Word Search>
   13.  Search Gopher Directory Titles via UNINETT... of Bergen  <Word Search>
   14.  Search Gopher Directory Titles via SCS Nevada             <Word Search
```

```
+———————————Search Gopher Directory Titles via U.Texas, Dallas———————————+>
|                                                                         |>
| Words to search for  earthquake                                         |>
|                                                                         |>
|                              [Cancel ^G] [Accept - Enter]               |>
|                                                                         |>
+—————————————————————————————————————————————————————————————————————————+>
```

```
 —> 1.  L.A. Earthquake Information                                <Directory>
     2.  94-earthquake                                             <Directory>
     3.  California, OES Earthquake Program                        <Directory>
     4.  Weather & Earthquake Information                          <Directory>
     5.  ***Northridge (LA) Earthquake Information ***             <Directory>
     6.  CALIFORNIA EARTHQUAKE EDIS Updates-Local EPIX archive     <Directory>
     7.  Caltech, Earthquake Engineering Laboratory (CALTECH)      <Directory>
     8.  ftp:lamont.columbia.edu : NCEER (Earthquake) - related..  <Directory>
     9.  Fault Lines - Earthquake Safety Updates                   <Directory>
    10.  L.A. Earthquake Information                                <Directory>
    11.2. Earthquake Information                                    <Directory>
    12. OKGEOSURVEY POSTSCRIPT SEISMOGRAMS v seismogram earthqu..   <Directory>
    13. Earthquake Information                                      <Directory>
    14. Earthquake Information Gopher                               <Directory>
    15. Caltech, Earthquake Engineering Laboratory (CALTECH)       <Directory>
    16. Earthquake_Info                                            <Directory>
    17. Northridge Earthquake                                      <Directory>
    18. Earthquake Information                                     <Directory>
```

Example of Jughead Search:

```
        OhioLINK: Ohio Library and Information Network

                  Search all of RiceInfo by title: Jughead

    1.  About this search of RiceInfo / About Jughead            <Text File>
 —> 2.  Search all of RiceInfo by title (jughead)                <Word Search>
```

```
+-------------Search all of RiceInfo by title (jughead)----------------------+
|                                                                            |
|  Words to search for   earthquake                                          |
|                                                                            |
|                              [Cancel ^G] [Accept - Enter]                  |
|                                                                            |
|                                                                            |
+-------------------------------------+--------------------------------------+
```

OhioLINK: Ohio Library and Information Network

Search all of RiceInfo by title (jughead): earthquake

—> 1.	Center for Earthquake Research and Information (CERI Me..	<Directory>
2.	Earthquake Information Gopher (NISEE)	<Directory>
3.	Earthquake Information	<Text File>
4.	Earthquake in Southwestern India—Sep. 30, 1993. From ..	<Text File>
5.	US National Earthquake Service Earthquake Lists	<Directory>
6.	Indian_earthquake	<Directory>
7.	Recent earthquake catalogs [FTP]	<Directory>
8.	Earthquake information from UWash (finger quake@geophys..	<Text File>
9.	Earthquake in India	<Text File>
10	QUAKELINE, National Center for Earthquake Engineering Rese..	<Telnet>

Bookmarks & Downloading in Gopher

Bookmarks

Going through several menu screens to reach your favorite resources each time you logon to Internet can be time consuming and frustrating, especially if you do not remember "the path" to the information. But there is relief: with an Internet account and gopher you can set bookmarks. In essence, you will be creating your own customized menu.

After you have created a bookmark list, there are two ways to get to your bookmark menu. This depends on how you gain access to the Internet. If you are in a UNIX shell with a system prompt, you type **gopher -b**. If you are already in a gopher system, simply type **v** to view your bookmarks. Once you retrieve your bookmark menu, use the arrow key to point and go. You will then see the menu for the Internet site you chose from your bookmark list.

How to Make a Bookmark List

Bookmarks are added and saved in the exact order you mark them. If you want your bookmarks in alphabetical order, you must enter them that way. Here is how you do it:

Step 1. Enter your gopher system.
Step 2. Go through the menu screens until you reach on of your favorite Internet sites such as NASA SpaceLINK and point to it.
Step 3. Type a lower case **a**. This will add the item to your bookmark list. Type an upper case **A** to add the entire directory.
Step 4. Type a name for the item or press return to use the one on the screen.
Step 5. Add other sites.
Step 6. Type **v** to view and access your bookmark list if you are in gopher; type **gopher -b** if you are in a UNIX shell.
Step 7. If you want to delete an entry from your bookmark list, point to the entry and type **d**.

Bookmarks are saved in a resource file (.gopherrc) in your Internet account. This file contains the gopher addresses and paths needed to connect to the Internet sites you chose for your bookmark list. The .gopherrc file will not show up in the directory listing on your account because the dot in front of the filename makes the file "invisible." To view the contents of this file, type **more .gopherrc** at the UNIX system prompt. You cannot view this file within the gopher program.

Pathways

One way to find places for setting your bookmarks is to follow pathways that others have already traveled. You must first navigate to a screen that says World Wide Gophers, Other Gopher Servers, or something similar, then follow the printed path. To reach the Library of Congress Gopher Server, you would follow this path:

World Wide Gophers/
   North America/
      USA/
         Washington D C/
            Library of Congress (LC MARVEL)

Downloading

Another great feature of the gopher system is the ability to download. Downloading is transferring a file from an Internet site across the telephone line to the hard drive on your personal computer. Before you begin the downloading process, you must read your telecommunications program manual and set the file type and transfer protocol. There are two file types for downloading: ASCII and binary. ASCII is used for text files and binary is used for image or program files. There are several transfer protocols: Kermit, Xmodem, Ymodem, and Zmodem. Kermit is the slowest while Zmodem is the fastest. Once you have configured these settings, you are ready to start downloading.

Step 1. Point to the name of the file you want to download. Be sure you have the correct file type chosen in your telecommunications program (either ASCII or binary).

Step 2. Type **shift - D** (uppercase D).

Step 3. You will see the screen listing the various types of transfer protocols. Select the protocol based on what you have set in your telecommunications program.

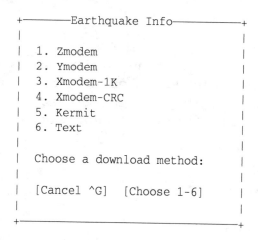

```
+------------Earthquake Info------------+
|                                       |
|   1. Zmodem                           |
|   2. Ymodem                           |
|   3. Xmodem-1K                        |
|   4. Xmodem-CRC                       |
|   5. Kermit                           |
|   6. Text                             |
|                                       |
|   Choose a download method:           |
|                                       |
|   [Cancel ^G]    [Choose 1-6]         |
|                                       |
+---------------------------------------+
```

Start your download now...

Step 4. Use the command in your telecommunications software, to receive the file. For example, in Procomm this is <PGDn>. You will not actually see the contents of the file. Rather, you will get a message similar to this:

```
Download Complete. 2754 total bytes, 45 bytes/sec
Press <RETURN> to continue
```

Step 5. To view the file you have just downloaded, use a word processor or graphics program and "retrieve" the file.

TELNET

Telnet allows you to logon to a remote host and interact as though you were actually sitting at that computer terminal.

To telnet:

At the system prompt > type telnet and the internet address

Example: **telnet spacelink.msfc.nasa.gov**

When initiating telnet sessions, sometimes you will have to know a login and password. Most lists or books containing telnet addresses, give this information. In some cases the host site will tell you the login and the password.

Example: login: NEWUSER
password: NEWUSER

The host may also ask for the type of terminal emulation you are using. The most commonly used type of terminal emulation is VT100.

Example: TERM = (unknown) > VT100

GENERAL TELNET STEP-BY-STEP INSTRUCTIONS:

Step 1. At the system prompt > type telnet internet address
        [ex. telnet spacelink.msfc.nasa.gov]
Step 2. login: type the login password [ex. visitor]
Step 3. TERM= (unknown) > **VT100** [terminal emulation]

If your screen freezes or you are unable to exit a telnet host, you can escape with these commands:

To escape telnet   1. type ^]   control-right bracket
                     2. telnet> **q**

HYTELNET

The Hytelnet program telnets for you and gives you the necessary information to logon to the system.

Example of Hytelnet Main Menu:

```
                    Welcome to HYTELNET
                        version 6.5
                      June 20, 1993

            What is HYTELNET?            <WHATIS>
            Library catalogs             <SITES1>
            Other resources              <SITES2>
            Help files for catalogs      <OP000>
            Catalog interfaces           <SYS000>
            Internet Glossary           <GLOSSARY>
            Telnet tips                  <TELNET>
            Telnet/TN3270 escape keys  <ESCAPE.KEY>
            Key-stroke commands           <HELP>

. . . . . . . . . . . . . . . . . . . . . . . . . . . . . . . . . . . . . . . .
Up/Down arrows MOVE      Left/Right arrows SELECT     ? for HELP anytime

            m  returns here        q  quits
. . . . . . . . . . . . . . . . . . . . . . . . . . . . . . . . . . . . . . . .

            HYTELNET 6.5 was written by Peter Scott
            E-mail address: aa375@freenet.carleton.ca
```

Select: **Other Resources**   **<Sites2>**

Select: **FREE-NETS & Community Computing Systems**

FREE-NETs & Community Computing Systems

\<FRE013\> Big Sky Telegraph
\<FRE012\> Buffalo FREE-NET
\<FRE022\> CapAccess: National Capital Area Public Access Network
\<FRE001\> Cleveland FREE-NET
\<FRE023\> Columbia Online Information Network (COIN)
\<FRE011\> Denver FREE-NET
\<FRE002\> Heartland FREE-NET
\<FRE008\> Lorain County FREE-NET
\<FRE017\> National Capital Freenet, Ottawa, Canada
\<FRE015\> SENDIT
\<FRE020\> Tallahassee Free-Net
\<FRE025\> Traverse City Free-Net
\<FRE005\> Tri-State Online (Cincinnati)
\<FRE021\> Vaasa FreePort Bulletin Board (BBS)
\<FRE018\> Victoria FREE-NET
\<FRE024\> Virginia's Public Education Network
\<FRE014\> Wellington Citynet
\<FRE003\> Youngstown FREE-NET

Select: CapAccess: National Capital Area Public Access Network

CapAccess: National Capital Area Public Access Network

TELNET CAP.GWU.EDU or 128.164.140.32
login: **guest**
Password: **visitor**

CapAccess Main Menu

1 Administration - User Services
2 Post Office - Email, User Directories
3 Public Forums
4 Media Center
5 Government Center
6 Education Center
7 Social Services Center
8 Libraries
9 Health Center
10 Community Center
11 Sports and Recreation Center
12 Arts and Entertainment Center
13 Business and Professional Center
14 Science and Technology Center
15 Policy Center

To end telnet:

Ending a telnet session depends on the commands of the host system. Some examples for logging out are quit, exit, bye, goodbye, and logoff. On some systems you will be able to choose the exit command from a menu.

W_{AIS}

A WAIS or wide area information server allows you to search indexed databases for information. Some WAIS servers are better than others.

WAIS STEP-BY-STEP INSTRUCTIONS:

Step 1. At the system prompt > type **telnet sunsite.unc.edu**
Step 2. login: **swais**
Step 3. TERM = (unknown) **vt100**
Step 4. Select the database to search by pressing the space bar.
Step 5. Type **w** for keyword.
Step 6. Keywords: type in the keywords
Step 7. Use the arrow key to move to your selection then press the space bar.
Step 8. Press the return key to view the document.

Example of a WAIS Search:

> **telnet sunsite.unc.edu**
...Trying 152.2.22.81...
Connected to SUNSITE.UNC.EDU.
Escape character is '^]'.

*********************** Welcome to SunSITE.unc.edu ***********************

SunSITE offers several public services via login. These include:

For a simple gopher client,	login as gopher
For a simple World Wide Web client,	login as lynx
For a simple WAIS client (over 500 databases),	login as swais
For WAIS search of political databases,	login as politics
For WAIS search of LINUX databases,	login as linux

For an FTP session, ftp to sunsite.unc.edu. Then login as anonymous

For more information about SunSITE, send mail to info@sunsite.unc.edu

SunOS UNIX (calypso)

login: **swais**

you're probably a vt100 or should be
TERM = (unknown) **vt100**
It takes a minute to load all the database information

```
SWAIS                     Source Selection                    Sources: 646
 #          Server                      Source                        Cost
073:    [          archie.au]     archie.au-ls-1Rt                    Free
074:    [          archie.au]     archie.au-mac-readmes               Free
075:    [          archie.au]     archie.au-pc-readmes                Free
076:  [askhp.ask.uni-karlsr]     ASK-SISY-Software-Information        Free
077:    [       ericir.syr.edu]   AskERIC-Helpsheets                  Free
078:    [       ericir.syr.edu]   AskERIC-Infoguides                  Free
079:  * [      ericir.syr.edu]   AskERIC-Lesson-Plans                Free
080:    [       ericir.syr.edu]   AskERIC-Minisearches                Free
081:    [       ericir.syr.edu]   astropersons                        Free
083:    [ cast0.ast.cam.ac.uk]   astroplaces                         Free
084:    [          archie.au]     au-directory-of-servers             Free
085:    [    doppler.ncsc.org]   AVS_TXT_FILES                       Free
086:    [        wais.eff.org]   bcs-calendar                        Free
087:  [ndadsb.gsfc.nasa.gov]     BGRASS-L                            Free
088:    [      wais.fct.unl.pt]   bib-appia                           Free
089:    [    cirm2.univ-mrs.fr]   bib-cirm                            Free
090:    [       snekkar.ens.fr]   bib-dmi-ens-fr                      Free
```

Keywords: **puzzles**

<space> selects, w for keywords, arrows move, <return> searches, q quits, or ?

```
SWAIS                          Search Results                    Items:   5
  #    Score  Source                            Title                Lines
001: *[1000] (          lessons)  cecmath.06  /ftp/pub/AskERIC/FullText/L   116
002:  [ 700] (          lessons)  cecmath.22  /ftp/pub/AskERIC/FullText/L    90
003:  [ 300] (          lessons)  Math-INDEX  /ftp/pub/AskERIC/FullText/     79
004:  [ 200] (          lessons)  cecmath.34  /ftp/pub/AskERIC/FullText/L    97
005:  [ 100] (          lessons)  cecmisc.21  /ftp/pub/AskERIC/FullText/L    74
```

WORLD WIDE WEB

The World Wide Web is a hypertext based program which creates links or jumping points to resources such as documents, pictures, sounds, or video clips. You navigate through these links using either a text or graphical browser. With a text browser, you highlight text and use your arrow keys. With a graphical browser, you point and click on the highlighted text or boxes.

World Wide Web includes links to hypertext media, gopher, FTP, telnet, hytelnet, Usenet news groups, WAIS, and other documents. A World Wide Web address on the Internet is called a URL (Uniform Resource Locator). Here is an example of the URL for AskERIC's gopher and web sites :

gopher://ericir.syr.edu:70/11/
http://ericir.syr.edu

Gopher and http (hypertext transfer protocol) tell you the access method. The information after the colon tells you the machine name, port numbers, and path. It is important to know URLs when you want to manually go to a site.

The language used to create hypertext documents is called HTML (Hypertext Markup Language). Home Pages are created by information providers or web servers as starting points to their resources using HTML. People in charge of their web are called WebMasters. For more information about the web, read *World Wide Web Frequently Asked Questions* available via ftp at rtfm.mit.edu in /pub/usenet/news.answers/www/faq or from Usenet newsgroups under news.answers.

If you would like to set up a Macintosh web server in your classroom, read the *Classroom Internet Server Cookbook* written by Stephen E. Collins at URL: http://web66.coled.umn.edu/Cookbook/contents.html.

Graphical Browsers

To use a graphical browser you must be directly connected to the Internet as a TCP/IP node, or a SLIP or PPP connection; use a 9600 baud modem or higher; and run a Macintosh with System 7 or greater or a PC with Microsoft Windows (16-bit or 32-bit). Several browsers are available free of charge on the Internet. In addition, you will also need helper applications for viewing and listening.

Windows

Cello
ftp.law.cornell.edu in /pub/LII/cello

Mosaic for Windows
ftp.ncsa.uiuc.edu in /PC/Windows/Mosaic

Netscape
ftp.mcom.com in /netscape/

WinWeb
ftp.einet.net in /einet/pc/winweb

Lview31.zip (to view JPEG images)
archive.umich.edu in /windows/graphicslview31.zip

MPEG (to view movies)
gatekeeper.dec.com in /pub/micro/msdos/win3/desktop/
mpegwin.zip

Wham1.31 (to listen to audio)
gatekeeper.dec.com in /pub/micro/win3/sounds/
wham131.zip

Macintosh

Mosaic for Macintosh
ftp.ncsa.uiuc.edu in Mac/Mosaic/

MacWeb
ftp.einet.net in einet/mac/macweb/

Netscape
ftp.mcom.com in/netscape/

Samba
info.cern.ch in /ftp/pub/www/bin

JPEGview 3.3 (to view JPEG images)
ftp.utexas.edu in pub/mac/graphics/JPEGview3.3.hqx

Sparkle 2.3.1 (to view movies)
ftp.utexas.edu in /pub/mac/graphics/sparkle-23-fat.hqx

Sound Machine 2.1 (to listen to audio)
ftp.utexas.edu in /pub/mac/util/soundmachine-21.hqx

Netscape

Netscape is an example of a graphical browser for the World Wide Web and is distributed by Netscape Communications Corporation in Mountain View, California. The company was founded in April, 1994, by Jim Clark, who was once Chairman of Silicon Graphics, and by Marc Andreesen, who developed the idea for the Mosaic interface.

Searching on the Web

How do you find information or locations on the World Wide Web? The "Hot List" appears on Mosaic, while Netscape has What's New and What's Cool. There are also other tools that search documents, titles, indexes, and directories. There are no search engines that have everything on the web, nor are they equally effective in their retrieval rates. Experimenting with several is the best approach.

Search Engines

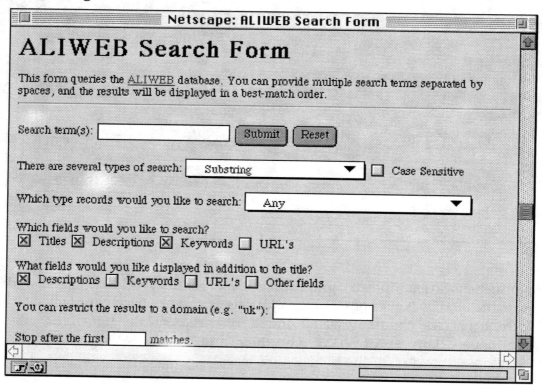

ALIWEB
http://web.nexor.co.uk/aliweb/doc/aliweb.html

Netscape: Lycos Search Form

Lycos™

Lycos Search Form

Query: [   ] [Search]

Terms to Match: [Any (OR) ▼]   **Number of Results:** [10 ▼]

Output Level: [Verbose ▼]

- Search language help
- Formless Interface
- Back to the Lycos Home Page.

The Lycos(tm) "Catalog of the Internet" copyright © 1994, 1995 Carnegie-Mellon University.
All rights reserved.

The Lycos Search Page
http://lycos.cs.cmu.edu

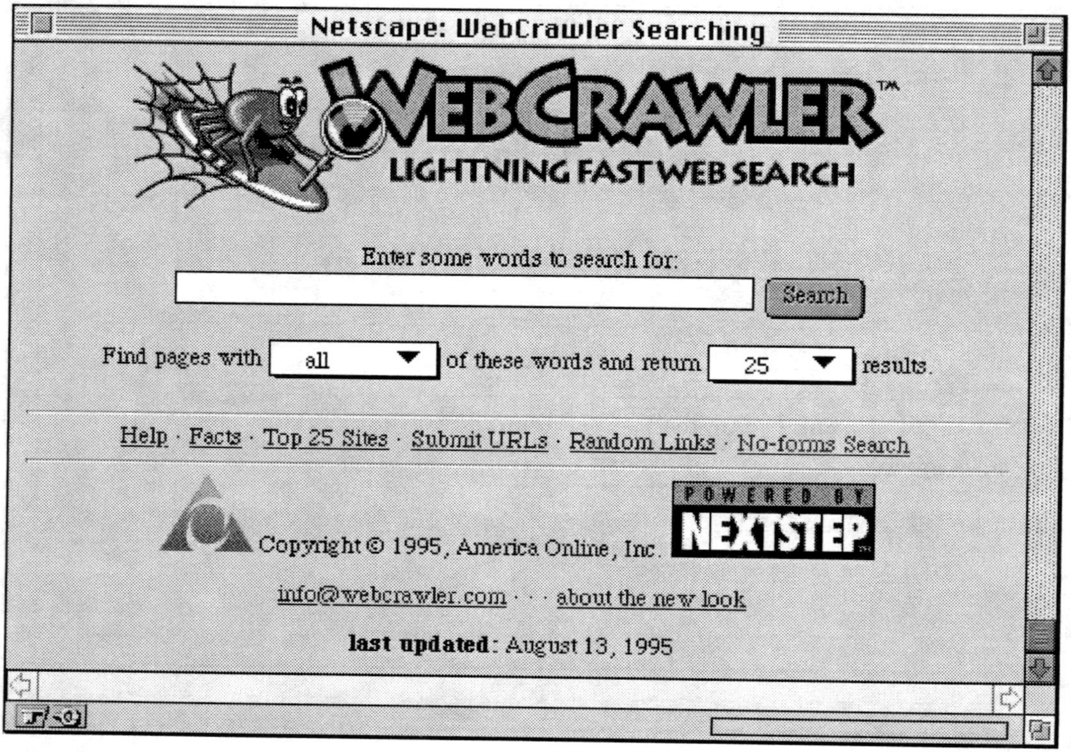

WebCrawler Searching
http://webcrawler.com

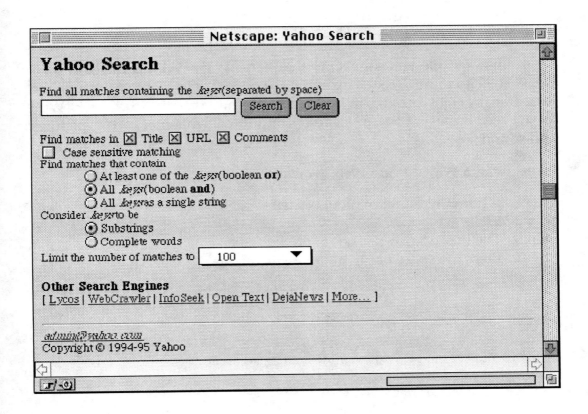

Yahoo
http://beta.yahoo.com/search.html

Text Based Browser in a UNIX Shell

In this example you connect to the World Wide Web via telnet in your UNIX shell account. Use the up and down arrow keys to move through the text. Use the right arrow to follow a link and the left arrow to go back. With a text based browser you cannot access multimedia material such as pictures and sound.

Example of a World Wide Web Browser Session:

Step 1. > **telnet ukanaix.cc.ukans.edu**
Step 2. login: **www**
Step 3. The menu below is shown on the screen.
Press the space bar to go to the next page.

```
                                    Lynx default home page (p1 of 2)

                  WELCOME TO LYNX AND THE WORLD OF THE WEB

You are using a WWW Product called Lynx. For more information about
obtaining and installing Lynx please choose About Lynx

The current version of Lynx is 2.1.1. If you are running an earlier
version PLEASE UPGRADE! Lynx version 2.2 is now in Beta.

INFORMATION SOURCES ABOUT AND FOR WWW
     * For a description of WWW choose Web Overview
     * About the WWW Information Sharing project
     * WWW Information By Subject
     * WWW Information By Type


OTHER INFO SOURCES
     * University of Kansas CWIS
     * O'Reilly & Ass. Global Network Navigator
     * Nova-Links: Internet access made easy
     * NCSA: Network Starting Points, Information Resource Meta-Index
  Arrow keys: Up and Down to move. Right to follow a link; Left to go back.
    O)ptions P)rint G)o M)ain menu Q)uit /=search [delete]=history list
Type a command or ? for help:                    Press space for next page
```

Step 4. On page 2, use the down arrow key to highlight Astronomy and Astrophysics, then press the right arrow key to link.

```
    The World-Wide Web Virtual Library: Subject Catalogue (p2 of 8)
Archaeology
        Classics and Mediterranean Archaeology

Astronomy and Astrophysics
        Separate list.

<space> selects, arrows move, w for keywords, s for sources, ? for help
```

Step 5. Press the space bar to go to page 2. You will see the text below. Use the down arrow key to highlight space and press the right arrow key to link.

```
    The World-Wide Web Virtual Library: Astronomy and Astrophysics (p2 of
2)
        data and status information, California, USA)

    See also space .
```

Step 6. You will be linked to the screens below. Move the down arrow key to highlight NASA Headline News and press the right arrow key to link.

SPACE

Under construction. Omissions please to roeber@cern.ch.

* Answers to Frequently Asked Questions on sci.space
* National Aeronautics and Space Administration
* European Space Information System
* NASA Ames Research Center archives
* NASA Astrophysics Data System information
* NASA Astrophysics Data System user guide
* NASA JPL FTP archive
* NASA Langley techreports (directory)
* NASA Langley techreports (searchable)
* NASA Spacelink (interactive session)
* National Space Science Data Center Online Data and Information Service (interactive session)
* Space Telescope Science Institute electronic information service
* Space Telescope – European Coordinating Facility STARCAT archive (interactive session)

Press space for next page

* Voyager, Hubble, and other images
* Yale Bright Star Catalog
* Orbital Element Sets: NASA, TVRO, Shuttle
* Orbital Element Sets: NASA, TVRO, Molczan, CelBBS, Shuttle
* Orbital Element Sets: NASA, Molczan
* Back issues of the Electronic Journal of the Astronomical Society of the Atlantic
* **NASA Headline News**
* NASA Extragalactic Database
* National Oceanic and Atmospheric Administration database
* Vincent Cate's list of companies related to the space industry
* Skywatch
* Frequently Seen Acronyms
* Daily Ionospheric Reports
* Delta Clipper images
* Space Digest archives: Current volume and Ancient volumes
* Space Tech archives (afs)
* Lunar and Planetary Institute BBS (interactive)
* USGS Global Land Information System BBS (interactive)
* Auroral activity images

Step 7. You will receive information for that date.

NASANEWS@SPACE.MIT.EDU [IMAGE] [IMAGE]

nasanews: [space] Wed Jan 19 23:27:54 1994

MIT Center for Space Research

If you have any suggestions for how we might improve this service,
please mail them to "nasanews@space.mit.edu". We regret that we are
NOT able to send bulletins to you via email. They are ONLY available
by tcp/finger. Note that NASA bulletins are frequently posted to the
"sci.space" and "sci.space.news" newsgroups and some are also stored
on the "explorer.arc.nasa.gov" ftp server. We also maintain an email
listserver at "pds-listserver@space.mit.edu" and a WWW server whose
URL is "http://delcano.mit.edu/".

C O N T E N T S

1 Wed Jan 19 10:29   KSC Shuttle Status

Date: Wed Jan 19 10:29:00 1994
Subject: KSC SHUTTLE STATUS REPORT 1/19/93

KENNEDY SPACE CENTER SPACE SHUTTLE STATUS REPORT

MISSION: STS-60 — WAKE SHIELD FACILITY AND SPACEHAB 2

% VEHICLE: Discovery/ OV-103	ORBITAL ALTITUDE: 218 sm
% LOCATION: Pad 39-A	INCLINATION: 57 degrees
% TARGET LAUNCH DATE: February 3	CREW SIZE: 6
% MISSION DURATION: 8 days/ 5 hours	WINDOW: 2 hours, 30 minutes

```
IN WORK TODAY:

* Loading of hypergolic propellants/ launch pad closed for routine work
* Recheck of data from Wake Shield Facility Interface Verification Test


WORK SCHEDULED:
                                          Finger Gateway (p3 of 3)

* Loading of hypergolic propellants will continue until late Thursday
evening or very early Friday morning * Retest of open items from
payload Interface Verification Test


WORK COMPLETED:

* Payload Interface Verification Test * Payload bay doors closed for
hypergolic fuel loading * X-ray of main engine hydraulic line quick
disconnect * Helium Signature leak check
```

Example of a Direct Connection with Lynx:

You can also go directly to a site if you know the URL.

Step 1. To go to a specific site, type **g**.
Step 2. At the **URL to open:** prompt, type the address.

```
       URL to open:http://www.enc.org
```

Bookmarking in Lynx

Step 1. To set a bookmark, highlight the site and type **a**.
Step 2. Choose l to link to the bookmark file.
Step 3. To view your bookmark list within lynx, type **v**.

To delete the bookmark, highlight the item and type **r**.

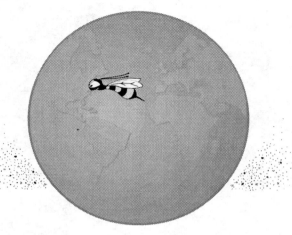

CHAPTER 4

Electronic Publishing

Publishing on the Net

You can initiate projects and share ideas on the Internet by becoming an information provider.

Tips For Getting Started

- Find a place to post your information such as your school server or an Internet provider that is directly connected to the Internet.

- Decide how elaborate you want the information to look on the net. It is easy to post text. More time and effort are involved with images, sound, and video.

- Decide whether you want to post information on a gopher or the World Wide Web. You can create text based information for gopher using a word processing program and saving it as an ASCII text file. If you want to create files for the World Wide Web, you will need to know how to write in HTML (Hypertext Markup Language). It is not difficult to learn and will give your information added flair when you include color icons, images, sound, and video.

- Carefully plan what information you want to share with others and how it will be arranged for easy access and understanding.

- Consider using an HTML editor or converter to prepare information for the World Wide Web.

  Some good sources for web publishing:

  http://www.yahoo.com/Computers/World_Wide_Web/
  http://online.anu.edu.au/CNIP/authors/
  http://www.webcom.com/~webcom/html/

  Teach Yourself Web Publishing with HTML in a Week by Laura Lemay and published by SAMS Publishing is a very comprehensive source with lots of examples and exercises to follow.

Style Guide for Text

- Use a monospace type such as Courier.
- Use 10 point type.
- Line length should not exceed 72 characters (1 inch left margin and 1.5 inch right margin).
- Maintain block style paragraphs with no indentations.
- Maintain a ragged right with no justification.
- Double-space between paragraphs.
- Use spaces instead of tabs to create columns.
- Do not use any special characters.
- Save the file as a text file with character returns at the end of each line.

Example:

```
    SCHOOL NEWSLETTER Vol. 1 No.1 Date

Welcome to the first edition of our electronic newsletter.  We
have lots of information to share about our school and the
projects we are doing in science and language arts.

***

Science Class

Last Friday we spent an overnight at school working on the Egg-A-
Thon project with our partner school in Hawaii.  We e-mailed with
them, sent them a raw egg in a package we designed from cardboard
and tape, and sent them a decorated egg with pictures about our
city and state.  It was a lot of fun. Our teacher's name was
Eggbeater.
                         Jason, 5th Grade Reporter
```

HTML

Hypertext Markup Language formats items in a document so they will appear in a specific way on the screen when using a World Wide Web browser. It is also used to create links to other documents or locations. HTML uses tags to do this formatting. The tags work in pairs — one to begin < >, the other to end </>. Tags can be in either upper or lower case. You can use a word processing program or an HTML editor to construct a home page.

The following examples show how a page would appear in the Lynx and Netscape web browsers as well as the tags needed to create it. The tags are in bold. Explanations are below the text. The <html>, <head>, and <body> tags are optional within HTML documents, but recommended for the beginner.

Page in Lynx

                                          World Link   (p1   of 1)

                          Welcome to World Link

    Cyber Bee's Tips
    Reference
    Eisenhower National Clearinghouse

Page in Netscape

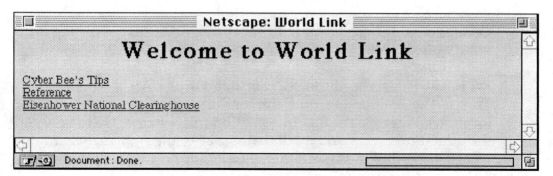

Tags

\<HTML\>
Begins the HTML Document

\<HEAD\>
Begins the Head of the Document

\<TITLE\>World Link\</TITLE\>
Creates the title you see in the upper right hand corner of the page or in the title bar of your web browser. Notice that < > begins the title and </> ends the title.

\</HEAD\>
Ends the HEAD information. The title is part of the main header.

\<BODY\>
Begins the document information. Most of the text, graphics, sound, video, and links are contained within the body of the document.

\<CENTER\>\<H1\>Welcome to World Link\</H1\>\</CENTER\>
There are actually two tags in this line — one to center the text and the other to denote the first level heading. There are different levels of headings with different point sizes.

\<P\>
Creates a paragraph break with space below the text. This tag does not require an end.

\<A HREF="cyberbee.html"\>Cyber Bee's Tips\</A\>
This is the anchor tag that creates links to other documents or locations. You type the link information (file name or URL) between the quotation marks and the link name after the right arrow. In this case you are linking to another file. Notice only the link name is visible on the page.

**
**
Creates a break with no space below the text.

<A HREF="gopher://nwoca7.nwoca.ohio.gov:70/ 11gopher_root%3A%5B_reference%5D">Reference</A>
 Creates a link to a gopher site.

**
**

<A HREF="http://www.enc.org">Eisenhower National Clearinghouse</A>
Creates a link to another web site.

</BODY>
Ends the body of the document.

</HTML>
Ends the HTML document.

10 Tips for WebMasters (Keep it simple, small, and short)

• Keep the size of your pages small. No one wants to wait 5 minutes for a page to load. Try to keep the load time within 30 seconds for your home page.

• Provide enough information on your home page so the reader will know about your location and what is available. Consider storyboarding your information before constructing your pages.

• Use courier or monaco 10 point for the body of the text. Save the file as text-only in a word processor with the extension .html or .htm on DOS. You can also use an HTML editor.

- Gif images should be no bigger than 20K. 2"x2" for a square or 1.5"x3" for a rectangle are good examples. Create thumbnail images that link to larger images on separate pages. Show the amount of K for each of the larger pictures so the reader will know the approximate load time.

- Keep in mind the width of the page when designing the size of logos. Readers will have various computer screen sizes. If the logo is too wide they will have to scroll in order to see all of it.

- Provide new information on a regular basis so readers will return. You might want to design interactive projects, links to changing information, or curriculum materials such as lesson plans.

- Avoid long lists of links to other sites.

- Each additional page should point back to the home page.

- Provide an e-mail address or contact information for comments from readers.

- Avoid publishing personal information.

HTML Tags

General Tags

\<html\>	\</html\>	complete HTML document
\<head\>	\</head\>	main header
\<title\>	\</title\>	title of the document
\<body\>	\</body\>	most of the document is included in the body

Headers

\<h1\>	\</h1\>	first level heading and most prominent
\<h2\>	\</h2\>	second level heading
\<h3\>	\</h3\>	third level heading
\<h4\>	\</h4\>	fourth level heading
\<h5\>	\</h5\>	fifth level heading
\<h6\>	\</h6\>	sixth level heading

Text

\<p\>		paragraph with space below the text
\<br\>		line break with no extra space below the text
\<hr\>		horizontal rule
\<pre\>	\</pre\>	preformatted text
\<em\>	\</em\>	emphasized text
\<blockquote\>	\</blockquote\>	quotation
\<dfn\>	\</dfn\>	definition
\<cite\>	\</cite\>	citation
\<b\>	\</b\>	bold
\<i\>	\</i\>	italics
\<u\>	\</u\>	underline
\<tt\>	\</tt\>	typewriter font

Image

`<img src="image.gif>`   designate a picture

Anchors

`<a href="URL">link name</a>`	link to another file
`<a name="target"</a>`	location in a document
`<a href="#anchor name">link name</a>`	link to a location in the same file
`<a href="URL#target"</a>`	link to a location in another file

Lists

Ordered List — Labeled with a Number Sequentially

`<ol>`	Begins a numbered list
`<li>`	First item will be labeled with a number 1
`<li>`	Next item will be labeled with a number 2
`</ol>`	Ends a numbered list

Unordered List — Preceded by a Bullet or Marker

`<ul>`	Begins a list that can be in any order
`<li>`	First item is preceded by a bullet or marker
`<li>`	Second item is preceded by a bullet or marker
`</ul>`	Ends the unordered list

Glossary List

`<dl>`	Begins the listing
`<dt>`	First term
`<dd>`	Term defined
`<dt>`	Second term
`<dd>`	Second term defined
`</dl>`	Ends the listing

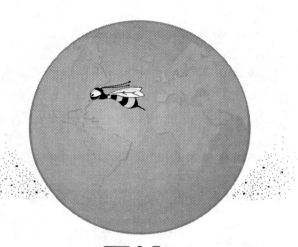

CHAPTER 5

File
Retrieval

Anonymous FTP

Anonymous FTP (file transfer protocol) allows you to transfer files from a remote computer to your account at your host site. Files are stored at the remote site in directories. To gain access to these files, you must initiate an anonymous ftp session and change directories, or type the directory path until you reach the file you want to transfer.

There are two types of files that can be transferred: ASCII and binary. The default setting is ASCII. Suppose you want to transfer the text file WWII.bib with a subdirectory path of /pub/research.guides from the Library of Congress. Here are the steps and screen examples for reading and transferring this file.

ASCII File Transfer

Step 1. At the system prompt > type **ftp** followed by the internet address of the remote ftp site (also called remote host).

Example: **ftp ftp.loc.gov**

```
{magnus jdoe 55} ftp ftp.loc.gov
Connected to rs7.loc.gov.
220 rs7 FTP server (Version 4.9 Thu Sep 2 20:35:07 CDT 1993) ready.
```

Once connected you will be asked to type in a user name. The user name is anonymous. The next prompt will ask for a password. The password is your e-mail address (example: jdoe@magnus.acs.ohio-state.edu). Sometimes the system will accept guest as the password.

Step 2. ```
Name (ftp.loc.gov:jdoe): anonymous
     331 Guest login ok, send ident as password.
```

Step 3.  ```
Password:guest
     230 Guest login ok, access restrictions apply.
```

Step 4. To see the main listing of what directories or files are on the system, you type **dir** or **ls** at the ftp prompt. The ls command lists the names of the files. The dir command gives a more complete description with file type, size, date, and name.

```
ftp> dir
200 PORT command successful.
150 Opening data connection for /bin/ls.
```

A list of other directories and files will be shown on the screen.

```
total 40
dr-xr-sr-x   2 root     system      512 Jan 14 14:42 bin
dr-xr-sr-x   2 root     system      512 Jan 14 14:47 etc
dr-xr-sr-x   2 root     system      512 Jan 14 14:42 lib
drwxrwsr-x  20 root     ftpa        512 Jun  2 17:23 pub
dr-xr-sr-x   3 root     system      512 Jan 14 14:42 usr
226 Transfer complete.
305 bytes received in 0.0039 seconds (76 Kbytes/s)
```

Step 5. To find the file WWII.bib you must change directories until the file is listed on the screen. To change directories, type **cd** or the directory path at the ftp prompt. Continue changing directories until you reach the file you want to transfer.

Example: ftp> **cd pub**
Example   ftp> **cd /pub/reference.guides**

Note: To go back up to the previous directory:

At the ftp> type **cd ..** or **cdup**

```
ftp> cd pub
250 CWD command successful.
```

To see the list under this directory type **dir**.

```
ftp> dir
200 PORT command successful.
150 Opening data connection for /bin/ls.
total 288
```

You will see these directories and files on the screen. Notice that files begin with - and directories begin with **dr**.

```
-rw-rw-r—    1 kell     ftpa       64648  May 25 13:57  INDEX
-rw-rw-r—    1 kell     ftpa        6339  Mar 11 16:20  README
drwxrwsr-x   7 kell     ftpa         512  Mar 28 13:43  client.software
drwxrwsr-x   2 emil     ftpa         512  Mar  7 16:25  collections.services
drwxrwsr-x   7 lbro     ftpa         512  Apr 20 09:40  exhibit.images
drwxrwsr-x   3 edel     ftpa         512  May 11 13:59  flicc
drwxrwsr-x   2 shal     ftpa         512  May 23 11:21  folklife
drwxrwsr-x   2 kell     ftpa         512  Mar 11 10:11  general.info
drwxrwsrwx   2 ldru     ftpa         512  Jun  3 11:18  incoming
drwxrwsr-x   3 ldru     ftpa         512  May 20 14:40  iug
drwxrwsr-x   2 cgia     ftpa         512  Apr 26 08:38  lc.access
drwxrwsr-x   2 rgue     ftpa         512  Mar  7 16:30  lc.classification
drwxrwsr-x   2 larr     ftpa         512  Mar  3 11:44  lc.online
drwxrwsr-x   2 ldru     ftpa         512  May 31 10:31  listproc
drwxrwsr-x   5 ldru     ftpa         512  Jun  2 17:34  nls
drwxrwsr-x   3 kell     ftpa         512  Mar 11 16:08  proceedings
drwxrwsr-x   2 larr     ftpa         512  May  3 14:56  reference.guides
drwxrwsr-x   3 kell     ftpa         512  Mar 11 16:02  utilities
drwxrwsr-x   5 jste     ftpa         512  Mar 11 16:02  viewers
drwxrwsr-x   2 ldix     ftpa         512  Jun  3 12:04  z3950
226 Transfer complete.
1321 bytes received in 0.28 seconds (4.7 Kbytes/s)
```

Since the file WWII.bib, is not listed you will need to change directories again.

This time change the directory to reference.guides.

```
ftp> cd reference.guides
250 CWD command successful.
```

To see the listing type **dir**.

```
ftp> dir
200 PORT command successful.
150 Opening data connection for /bin/ls.
total 584
```

In this directory you will see the text file WWII.bib listed.

```
-rw-rw-r—  1 larr     ftpa      56268 Mar  8 09:29 WWII.bib
-rw-rw-r—  1 larr     ftpa      83140 Mar  3 15:49 brit.govt.docs
-rw-rw-r—  1 tjab     ftpa      22332 May  3 14:56 stars.and.stripes
-rw-rw-r—  1 larr     ftpa      39502 Mar  3 15:49 us.govt.pubs
-rw-rw-r—  1 larr     ftpa      87933 Mar  3 15:49 us.legis.docs
226 Transfer complete.
355 bytes received in 0.012 seconds (30 Kbytes/s)
```

Since the file to be transferred is an ASCII text file, you can read the file prior to transferring it to your local site. To read a text file.

At the ftp> type **get filename | more**

```
ftp> get WWII.bib |more
200 PORT command successful.
150 Opening data connection for WWII.bib (56268 bytes).
226 Transfer complete.
```

Step 6. Now you are ready to transfer the WWII.bib file.

> At the ftp> type **get filename**

```
ftp> get WWII.bib
200 PORT command successful.
150 Opening data connection for WWII.bib (56268 bytes).
226 Transfer complete.
local: WWII.bib remote: WWII.bib
57691 bytes received in 3.2 seconds (17 Kbytes/s)
```

Step 7. The file was successfully transferred and you are ready to exit the ftp session. To end an ftp session:

> At the ftp> type **bye**

```
ftp> bye
221 Goodbye.
```

Step 8. To list the file at your local site:

> At the system prompt> type **ls** or **dir** depending on your local system commands.

> Example: > **ls**

Step 9. To read a transferred text file at you local site:

> At the system prompt > type **more filename**.

> Example: > **more WWII.bib**

Binary File Transfer

To transfer binary files, you must indicate the file type at the ftp prompt. Suppose you want the file SHARKS.GIF with subdirectory path /images/gif89a/new-photo-uploads located at the Smithsonian FTP site. Here are the step-by-step instructions and menu screens for transferring this binary file:

Step 1. At the system prompt >   type **ftp** followed by the internet address of the remote ftp site (also called remote host).

```
{magnus jdoe 51} ftp photo1.si.edu
Connected to photo1.si.edu.
220 photo1.si.edu FTP server (Version 5.152 Fri May 14 15:21:57 PDT 1993) ready.
```

Once connected you will be asked to type in a user name. The user name is anonymous. The next prompt will ask for a password. The password is your e-mail address. Sometimes the system will accept guest as the password.

Step 2. `Name (photo1.si.edu:jdoe):` **anonymous**
            `331 Guest login ok, send ident as password.`
Step 3. `Password:`**guest**
            `230 Guest login ok, access restrictions apply.`

Step 4. To see the listing of what directories or files are on the system, type **dir** or **ls** at the ftp prompt.

```
ftp> dir
200 PORT command successful.
150 Opening ASCII mode data connection for /bin/ls.
total 52
```

A list of other directories and files will be shown on the screen.

```
-rw-r—r—        1 root    bin      1358   Oct 23  1992  ALOT-Chapman.txt
drwxr-xr-x      3 root    root      512   Jan 28 18:08  More.Smithsonian.Stuff
-rw-r—r—        1 root    bin      6147   Dec 11  1992  SMITHSONIAN.RULES.TXT
drwxr-xr-x      5 root    bin       512   Feb 14 12:18  apps
d—x—x—x         2 root    root      512   Oct  5  1992  bin
d—x—x—x         2 root    root      512   Jun  1  1993  etc
drwxr-xr-x      8 root    root      512   Jun  2 13:15  images
d—x—x—x         8 root    root      512   Jun  7 20:42  pub
d—x—x—x         2 root    bin       512   Oct  5  1992  shlib
226 Transfer complete.
679 bytes received in 0.28 seconds (2.4 Kbytes/s)
```

Step 5. To find the file SHARKS.GIF you must change directories until the file is listed on the screen. To change directories, type **cd** or the directory path at the ftp prompt.

```
ftp> cd images

ftp> cd gif89a
250 CWD command successful.

ftp> dir
200 PORT command successful.
150 Opening ASCII mode data connection for /bin/ls.
total 36
drwxr-xr-x 2 root      root     2048   Jun  9 13:11  air-space
drwxr-xr-x 2 root      root     1024   Apr 21 15:22  art
drwxr-xr-x 2 root      root     2560   Jun  9 13:12  new-photo-uploads
drwxr-xr-x 2 root      root     4096   Jun  9 13:09  people-places
drwxr-xr-x 2 root      root     4096   Jun  9 13:11  science-nature
drwxr-xr-x 2 root      root     3584   Jun  9 13:11  tech-history
226 Transfer complete.
414 bytes received in 0.039 seconds (10 Kbytes/s)
```

```
ftp> cd new-photo-uploads
250 CWD command successful.

ftp> dir
200 PORT command successful.
150 Opening ASCII mode data connection for /bin/ls.
total 7928
-rw-r-r-   1 root     root       184955  May 26 11:30 2NDDIV.GIF
-rw-r-r-   1 root     root       118832  May 26 11:30 442ND.GIF
-rw-r-r-   1 root     root       140163  May 26 11:30 A4C.GIF
-rw-r-r-   1 root     root       216621  May 26 11:30 AIDS.GIF
-rw-r-r-   1 root     root       138525  May 26 11:30 ALLOSR.GIF
-rw-r-r-   1 root     root       168805  May 26 11:30 ARLTON.GIF
-rw-r-r-   1 root     root       157619  May 26 11:30 BLENNY.GIF
-rw-r-r-   1 root     root       175025  May 26 11:30 BRADLY.GIF
-rw-r-r-   1 root     root       230748  May 18 11:11 GULF.GIF
-rw-r-r-   1 root     root       231940  May 18 11:12 HUBBLE.GIF
-rw-r-r-   1 root     root       199345  May 18 11:12 INDY02.GIF
-rw-r-r-   1 root     root       122627  May 18 11:12 JEFSON.GIF
-rw-r-r-   1 root     root       178995  May 18 11:12 JFKCTR.GIF
-rw-r-r-   1 root     root       180398  May 18 11:12 KBEES.GIF
-rw-r-r-   1 root     root       104998  May 18 11:12 KVULTR.GIF
-rw-r-r-   1 root     root       161852  May 25 13:00 POTTRY.GIF
-rw-r-r-   1 root     root        11457  Jun  8 16:40 REDCLDTP.GIF
-rw-r-r-   1 root     root       116755  May 25 13:00 SAO01.GIF
-rw-r-r-   1 root     root        88381  May 25 13:00 SAO02.GIF
-rw-r-r-   1 root     root       152064  May 25 13:00 SAO03.GIF
-rw-r-r-   1 root     root       152856  May 25 13:00 SAO04.GIF
-rw-r-r-   1 root     root       127047  May 25 13:00 SAO05.GIF
-rw-r-r-   1 root     root       115215  May 25 13:00 SAO06.GIF
-rw-r-r-   1 root     root       229769  May 25 13:00 SHARKS.GIF
-rw-r-r-   1 root     root        19710  Jun  8 16:40 SKYLB1TP.GIF
-rw-r-r-   1 root     root        21288  Jun  8 16:40 SLOTHTP.GIF
-rw-r-r-   1 root     root        17915  Jun  8 16:40 SUBTP.GIF
-rw-r-r-   1 root     root        14219  Jun  8 16:40 TBEARTP.GIF
226 Transfer complete.
1850 bytes received in 0.28 seconds (6.5 Kbytes/s)
```

Step 6. To transfer a binary file, you must indicate the file type.

   At the ftp> type **binary**

```
ftp> binary
200 Type set to I.
```

Step 7. Now you are ready to transfer the SHARKS.GIF file.

   At the ftp> type **get filename**

```
ftp> get SHARKS.GIF
200 PORT command successful.
150 Opening BINARY mode data connection for SHARKS.GIF (229769 bytes).
226 Transfer complete.
local: SHARKS.GIF remote: SHARKS.GIF
229769 bytes received in 7.9 seconds (29 Kbytes/s)
```

Step 8. The file was transferred successfully and you are ready to quit the ftp session.

   At the ftp> type **bye**

```
ftp> bye
221 Goodbye.
```

ARCHIE

Archie allows you to search for files at anonymous ftp sites. The Archie database is updated about once a month. If your host does not have a menu driven Archie server, telnet to one that does.

ARCHIE STEP-BY-STEP INSTRUCTIONS:

Step 1. At the system prompt > type **telnet** to an archie site.
> [ex. telnet archie.sura.net]

Step 2. login: **archie** or **qarchie** depending on the host site.

Step 3. At the system prompt > **prog filename** [type the keyword].

Step 4. Results of the search will be displayed with a **:** at the end of each page.
At the **:** prompt, press the space bar to view the next page of results.

Step 5. Type **q** to search another filename.
Type **quit** to exit the archie program.

Example of an Archie Search:

```
> telnet archie.sura.net
Trying 128.167.254.195...

SunOS UNIX (yog-sothoth.sura.net)

login: qarchie
Last login: Tue Jan 18 12:06:59 from Huskyl.StMarys.C
SunOS Release 4.1.3 (NYARLATHOTEP) #3: Thu Apr 22 15:26:21 EDT 1993

>prog whitehouse
Processing Case Insensitive Substring Search for 'whitehouse'

Host 130.149.17.7

     Location: /pub/amiga/uni-kl/aminet/mods/8voic
        FILE -rw-rw-r—    56541  Apr 26 1993    AtTheWhiteHouse.lha
        FILE -rw-rw-r—     1007  Apr 26 1993    AtTheWhiteHouse.readme

Host life.anu.edu.au

     Location: /pub/general/fun
        FILE -rw-rw-rw-   16105  Jun  8 00:00   whitehouse.faq
```

: [At the prompt, press space bar to view the next page of results]

```
END quit
```

LIST OF ARCHIE SERVERS

The following is a list of other Archie servers:

archie.ans.net	147.225.1.10	(ANS server, NY (USA))
archie.au	139.130.4.6	(Australian Server)
archie.doc.ic.ac.uk	146.169.11.3	(United Kingdom Server)
archie.edvz.uni-linz.ac.at	140.78.3.8	(Austrian Server)
archie.funet.fi	128.214.6.102	(Finnish Server)
archie.internic.net	198.49.45.10	(AT&T server, NY (USA))
archie.kr	128.134.1.1	(Korean Server)
archie.kuis.kyoto-u.ac.jp	130.54.20.1	(Japanese Server)
archie.luth.se	130.240.18.4	(Swedish Server)
archie.ncu.edu.tw	140.115.19.24	(Taiwanese server)
archie.nz	130.195.9.4	(New Zeland server)
archie.rediris.es	130.206.1.2	(Spanish Server)
archie.rutgers.edu	128.6.18.15	(Rutgers University (USA))
archie.sogang.ac.kr	163.239.1.11	(Korean Server)
archie.sura.net	128.167.254.195	(SURAnet server MD (USA))
archie.sura.net(1526)	128.167.254.195	(SURAnet alt. MD (USA))
archie.switch.ch	130.59.1.40	(Swiss Server)
archie.th-darmstadt.de	130.83.22.60	(German Server)
archie.unipi.it	131.114.21.10	(Italian Server)
archie.univie.ac.at	131.130.1.23	(Austrian Server)
archie.unl.edu	129.93.1.14	(U. of Nebraska,Lincoln (USA))
archie.uqam.ca	132.208.250.10	(Canadian Server)
archie.wide.ad.jp	133.4.3.6	(Japanese Server)

Client software should be supported at all of these sites.

FILE MANAGEMENT

Files will often have an extension name attached. Many of these are compressed to save storage space and limit the download time. For example, .tar, .zip, and .sit can contain several small files within a larger file. Compressed files and files other than text will need software to uncompress and run them.

MS-DOS

Files ending in .exe or .com need no decompression, and are ready to run simply by typing the name. To uncompress .arc or .zip files, you will need the shareware utility programs PKarc and PKzip by PKWare Inc. PKUNZIP is part of the PKzip package.

PKzip204g.exe
　　　　ftp.virginia.edu in /pub/pc

Uncompressing a .zip file:

Step 1. Download the .zip file into the same directory as PKUNZIP.
Step 2. Type PKUNZIP and the name of the downloaded file.
Step 3. The file will be uncompressed and you will have a program ready to run.

Macintosh

The commercial software program Stuffit Deluxe is one of the best packages for coding, decoding, stuffing, and unstuffing Macintosh files. There are also shareware and freeware programs on the Internet that can be used as well. BinHex is a shareware program for decoding .hqx files. Since many of the Macintosh programs on the Internet are stored in the BinHex format, this is an essential software program. There are three versions of BinHex: Version 4.0, a desk accessory version for 4.0, and Version 5.0. They are available via Anonymous FTP.

Binhex1.02.sit.hqx

      wuarchive.wustl.edu in /systems/mac/umich.edu/system.extensions/da

binhex4.0.bin

      archive.umich.edu in /mac/util/compression

Binhex_5..sea.hqx

      ftp.virginia.edu in /pub/mac/misc

To decode a .hqx file follow these steps.

Step 1. Get a .hqx file from an ftp site using **ASCII** file transfer.
Step 2. Download the file to your hard drive.
Step 3. Double click on the Binhex program [Tip: Make an alias of the program and put it in your Apple Menu. Then simply pull down to the program and it will launch.]
Step 4. Choose Download -> Application under the File Menu.
Step 5. Choose the .hqx file and place to save it.

Other Macintosh Compression Programs:

compact.pro1.34.sea.hqx

      archive.umich.edu in /mac/util/compression

stuffitexpander3.0.7.sea.hqx

      archive.umich.edu in /mac/util/compression

UNIX

UNIX files have the extension .Z attached to the filename. These files can be uncompressed at your host site. You can also compress files to save storage space.

At the system prompt> type **uncompress filename.Z**

      Example: **uncompress history.Z**

To compress a file to save storage space:

At the system prompt> type **compress filename**

Example: **compress history**

After compressing the file, it will have the .Z extension again.

.ps Files

The file extension .ps stands for postscript. This file can contain both graphics and text. It is encrypted to print on a postscript printer. Computer utility programs will send the information to a postscript printer.

GIF Files

GIF (pronounced jif) are universal graphics files. The format was developed by CompuServe to allow the same images to be seen on all types of computers. There are several good software programs for viewing .gif files on the Macintosh, DOS, and Windows platforms. Gifwatcher and Gif Converter are programs for the Macintosh, Showgif and Graphic Workshop are programs for MS-DOS, and LVIEW 3.1 and Graphic Workshop for Windows.

Macintosh

gifwatcher2.11.sit.hqx
   wuarchive.wustl.edu in /systems/mac/umich.edu/systems.extensions/da
gifconverter2.37.cpt.hqx
   archive.umich.edu in /mac/graphics/graphicsutil

MS-DOS

shwgif51.zip
   archive.umich.edu in /msdos/graphics/util
gifgrfwk70a.zip
   archive.umich.edu in /msdos/graphics/util

Windows

lview31.zip
  archive.umich.edu in /windows/graphics
gwswn11j.zip
  archive.umich.edu in /windows/graphics

One of the largest collections of GIF files can be found at Washington University of St. Louis. Another great site is the Smithsonian Institution.

ftp wuarchive.wustl.edu in /multimedia/images/gif
ftp photo1.si.edu in /images/gif89a

Guide For File Transfer

File Suffix	Transfer Type	Computer	Program
.bin	binary	Macintosh	executable
.cpt	binary	Macintosh	compact pro
.hqx	ASCII	Macintosh	BinHex
.sea	binary	Macintosh	self-extracting
.sit	binary	Macintosh	unstuffit
.gz	binary	UNIX	gunzip
.tar	binary	UNIX	tar command
.uue	ASCII	UNIX	uudecode command
.Z	binary	UNIX	uncompress
.arc	binary	PC	pkarc
.com	binary	PC	executable
.exe	binary	PC	executable
.zip	binary	PC	pkunzip
.gif	binary (graphics)	All	gif viewing programs
.ps	ASCII	All	postscript printer
.txt	ASCII	All	text editor

Downloading a File

The following are basic instructions for downloading files. There are several file transfer protocols, including Kermit, Xmodem, Ymodem, and Zmodem. Kermit is the slowest and Zmodem the fastest. Zmodem is currently the most common protocol. However, some UNIX hosts may support only Kermit.

Each telecommunications is slightly different. Refer to your program manual for the specifics.

Downloading A Text File With The Kermit Protocol

Macintosh & MacKermit Telecommunications Program

Step 1. At the system prompt > type **kermit**
Step 2. At the kermit prompt > type **send filename**
Step 3. When prompted for the receive command, go to the transfer menu and select receive file
Step 4. At the kermit prompt > type **quit**

PC & ProComm Telecommunications Program

Step 1. At the system prompt > type **kermit**
Step 2. At the kermit prompt > type **send filename**
Step 3. When prompted for the receive command, **press PGDn**, type **k** (for kermit) and press return/enter
Step 4. At the kermit prompt > type **quit**

Example:

{magnus jdoe 53} **kermit**
C-Kermit, 4F(095) 31 Aug 89, VAX/Ultrix
Type ? for help
C-Kermit>**send deer**
Escape back to your local Kermit and give a RECEIVE command...
C-Kermit> **quit**

Example on a VMS system:

```
$ kermit
VMS Kermit-32 version 3.3.128
Default terminal for transfers is: _CCA1110:
Kermit-32>send HUR
Kermit-32>quit
```

Downloading A Binary File With The Kermit Protocol

Macintosh & MacKermit Telecommunications Program

Step 1. At the system prompt > type **kermit**
Step 2. At the kermit prompt > type **set file type binary**
Step 3. At the kermit prompt > type **send filename**
Step 4. When prompted for the receive command, go to the transfer menu and select receive file
Step 5. At the kermit prompt > type **quit**

PC & ProComm Telecommunications Program

Step 1. At the system prompt > type **kermit**
Step 2. At the kermit prompt > type **set file type binary**
Step 3. At the kermit prompt > type **send filename**
Step 4. When prompted for the receive command, press **PGDn**, type **k** (for kermit) and press return/enter
Step 5. At the kermit prompt > type **quit**

Example on a UNIX system:

```
{magnus jdoe 53} kermit
C-Kermit, 4F(095) 31 Aug 89, VAX/Ultrix
Type ? for help
C-Kermit>set file type binary
C-Kermit>send quartz.gif
Escape back to your local Kermit and give a RECEIVE command...
C-Kermit> quit
```

119

Example on a VMS system:

$ kermit
VMS Kermit-32 version 3.3.128
Default terminal for transfers is: _CCA1110:
Kermit-32>**set file type binary**
Kermit-32>**send quartz.gif**
Kermit-32>**quit**

Downloading With Zmodem Protocol

To transfer a file from the host computer to your Macintosh or PC, you will use the command sz (send Zmodem) followed by either -a (ASCII text file) or -b (binary file).

Step 1. At the system prompt > type **sz -a filename**

or

Step 1. At the system prompt > type **sz -b filename**

Example on a Unix system:

> **sz -a Hurston.findingaid**

Either the file will be transferred automatically or a message may appear to receive the file. If the message appears, you must execute the command in your telecommunications program to receive the file.

Example on a VMS system:

$ sz -a HUR

*z
Receive (Z) hur: Exists, overwriting
Receive (Z) hur: 18513 bytes, 1:19 elapsed, 233 cps, 97%
$ .exe;3 3.12 04-11-91 finished.

CHAPTER 6

Internet in the
Classroom

CURRICULUM INFUSION USING THE BIG SIX SKILLS

Teaching information access skills cannot be done in a vacuum. It must relate to the learning environment by engaging students to gather and process information in a meaningful way. For example, a lesson on using a magazine index is soon forgotten if students are not involved in a related activity. However, teaching that same lesson while students are working on a project such as the different environmental habitats of animals brings that lesson to life. Students now understand that learning how to use the magazine index will help them find information about their chosen topic and successfully complete the project. It teaches them important critical thinking and problem solving skills.

Put the project in the context of the Big Six Skills, an approach to information problem solving developed by Michael B. Eisenberg and Robert E. Berkowitz. In this systematic method, Eisenberg and Berkowitz define six steps for resolving the initial problem.

1. Task Definition: determining the need for information

2. Information Seeking Strategies: examining alternative approaches to acquiring the appropriate information to meet defined tasks

3. Location and Access: locating information sources and information within sources

4. Use of Information: using a source to gain information

5. Synthesis: integrating information drawn from a range of sources

6. Evaluation: making judgments based on a set of criteria

How can the Internet be used as one of the tools in this process? To answer this question, look at Eisenberg's expanded Big Six Skills Chart which includes components for initiating activities and related features that are offered through the Internet. Using this as a guide, think about correlating e-mail with writing skills. Integrate information gathering for projects and reports with gopher, telnet, WAIS, and other Internet tools. When students process the information by reading, viewing, and listening, it helps them determine what materials are useful to solve a problem or answer a question. By sharing their reports and projects with others, students will gain valuable feedback for future learning.

After working through the capabilities and application suggestions from the chart, you can begin to construct a lesson plan. The sample lesson form is from the *Resource Companion to Curriculum Initiative: An Agenda and Strategy for Library Media Programs* by Michael B. Eisenberg and Robert E. Berkowitz. In this example, the study of animal habitat is adapted to the matrix of the Big Six Skills.

Within this context you become the facilitator and your students become collaborators with their peers. Not only will they learn valuable problem solving skills, but how to work together for common solutions. This helps prepare them to be world citizens in an information society.

Internet Capabilities in an Information Problem-Solving Context

The Big Six Skills	Internet Capability	Application
1. Task Definition		
1.1 Define the problem	E-mail	to seek clarification from teachers
1.2 Identify information requirements of the problem	E-mail	to consult with group/ team members
	Discussion/interest groups (listservs, newsgroups)	to share and discuss concerns/ questions/problems with persons in similar settings or with experts
2. Information seeking		
2.1 Determine the range of possible sources	Electronic libraries, data centers, resources	to be aware of options, to determine possible and priority sources
2.2 Evaluate to determine priority sources	WAIS, Gopher, various Internet resource guides	to determine possible resources, to search for types of files and data
	Use of AskERIC, NICs	to consult on resources, files, databases
	E-Mail	to consult with group/team members
	Electronic Discussion Groups (listservs, newsgroups)	to request recommendations from persons in similar settings or from experts
3. Location and Access		
3.1 Locate sources (intellectually), (physically)	Archie, Veronica	to search for the location of specific files or databases
3.2 Find information within sources	WAIS, Gopher	to search by subject within/across sites
	Telnet, Remote login, ftp	to obtain remote access to computers and electronic libraries
4. Use of Information		
4.1 Engage (read, view, listen)	Download and file transfer, ftp	to get the relevant information from a remote computer to your own
4.2 Extract relevant information		
5. Synthesis		
5.1 Organize information from multiple sources	E-Mail	to share drafts and final communications
5.2 Present Information	Listservs, newsgroups	to share papers, reports, and other communications
	Electronic Journals	to present papers and reports
	FTP and Gopher sites	to archive reports, papers, products
6. Evaluation		
6.1 Judge the product (effectiveness)	E-mail	to gain feedback
6.2 Judge the process (efficiency)	Listservs, newsgroups	to gain feedback

Source: Michael B. Eisenberg Educational Technology; v34 n7 Sept. 1994, p.63

LESSON PLAN

Date:

Subject: Science, Interdisciplinary   **Teacher:**   **Class:**

Lesson Name: Animal Habitat   **Location:**   **Time:** 3-4 weeks

Unit Context: Current Environmental Issues Between Man and Nature

Content Objectives: The student will be able to:
1. Recognize and identify the importance of animal habitat and adaptation on survival
2. Understand the impact of the industrial society on wildlife

Big Six Skills Objectives:	**Activities:**
1. Task:	1. Student Groups formed. General discussion for research.
2. Info seeking:	2. List information available - Be sure to include several types of media.
3. Location:	3. Library, local wildlife conservation facility: To include observation and inquiry.
4. Use of Information:	4. Examine resources from Internet , CD-ROM, books, magazine index; observe wildlife habitat at conservation site.
5. Synthesis:	5. Each student contributes his/her research to be included in the presentation. Each group will create a chart of the characteristics of their animal's habitat.
6. Evaluation:	6. Each group is responsible for a 10 minute re-cap of their findings to share with the entire class. A choice of notebook or multi media project will be required of each group.

Materials/Resources:

Animal Encyclopedias, Books on Animal Habitats, *Wild America* Videos, Internet (e-mail scientists with questions, retrieve pictures, articles (MVNWR lesson plans), read listservs on the topic), and visit a wildlife conservation facility.

Evaluation:

Self evaluation, peer review, and teacher

Notes: Each student will contribute their component to make a complete overview of animal habitat. The entire group makes an oral presentation to the class. The notebook or multimedia project will receive a group grade.

Getting Started

Imagine having your first cup of coffee before hitting the road for your commute to work. There in front of you is your laptop computer or message pad linked via phone to the computer network at school. You check on which of your students will be absent from school and assign their work with a personal greeting, "Hope you're feeling better." Then you check your e-mail to see what messages you need to answer immediately. The others can wait until later. You see there is a note from the curriculum coordinator who wants you to give a presentation to a group of teachers about the project you just completed with your history students using Internet resources. They researched a topic that was coming up for a vote in the House of Representatives. Then they debated the issue with their Congressional Representative via e-mail. You reply that you would love to bring some of your students to give their viewpoint on the project. Then you pack up your laptop and off you go.

This is what a school network might look like in the future. You may not be able to check on absences or send homework assignments now, but you can find information on upcoming Congressional bills and discuss the issue with one of the Congressional Representatives who has an e-mail address. What other things can you do until the day arrives when your school is completely wired to the technology envisioned for the twenty-first century? Here are a few suggestions to get you started.

Start with **e-mail**. This is a good way to introduce students to the Internet. One example is to correspond with another class either locally, nationally, or internationally. Perhaps senior citizens would like to be keypals with your students — one way to reach out to the community. E-mail can be incorporated into writing, social studies, language arts, or foreign language lessons. Once electronic messaging is mastered, students can correspond with field experts while working on project assignments. Many professionals such as authors, scientists, and artists are willing to help students via e-mail. Some examples include Ask A Scientist, Ask A Geologist, and Ask Dr. Math.

Access information on a **gopher** or **World Wide Web** system. Use these Internet tools as additional references for student research. Look at the *CIA World Factbook*, weather, and earthquake databases. Create a scavenger hunt to go along with a specific topic and provide lots of hints.

Participate in a project such as those provided through Academy One, NASA, and other organizations. Link up with other classrooms and create your own project. Check Kidsphere and other listservs for announcements.

Take time for yourself as a teacher to find curriculum materials by accessing the lesson plans located on AskERIC. Join a **listserv** and participate in lively discussions about topics of interest to you. Correspond with colleagues and exchange ideas.

Citing Electronic Resources

With access to information from a wide array of electronic services, one of the questions asked by teachers and students is how to reference resources from the Internet. The answer is the book *Electronic Style: A Guide to Citing Electronic Information* written by Xia Li and Nancy B. Crane and published by Meckler Publishing. It is very comprehensive in its scope and sequence. Each topic, such as electronic mail, FTP, telnet, and journals are shown with a basic form, then illustrated with several examples.

The basic form is used to cite the reference in such a way that the information can be found by others. Private e-mail correspondence is not accessible and some databases are only available by password or registered users. In either case, at least you will know where the reference originated.

It is important to cite the author, date, title, source, medium, and how the information is available. Here are some examples based on the style forms in the above work.

Basic form for citing individual works:

Author. (date). *Title* (edition), [Type of medium]. Available: give information sufficient for retrieval

E-Mail (Personal):

> Smith, Jane. (1995, January 10). *Holiday Highlights* [e-mail to ljoseph], [Online]. Available e-mail: ljoseph@osu.edu

E-Mail (Discussion Group or Listserv):

> Doe, Jane. (1995, January 10). *Acceptable Use Policy* [Discussion], LM_Net [Online]. Available e-mail: LM_Net@suvm.syr.edu

FTP:

Smith, Jennifer Moira. (1994, October 2). *Mud-Faq-P1*, [Online].
Available: FTP: ftp.math.okstate.edu Directory: pub/misc/mud-faq
File: mud-faq-p1

Gopher:

Adams, Martha. (1994, May 13). *M&M Math*, [Online]. Available:
Gopher: ericir.syr.edu Directory: Lesson Plans/Mathematics/
Using M&M Cookies to Work Math Problems (4-6) File:
cecmath.13

Telnet:

20/20 ABC (1992, December 18). Long Journey Home. In *Journal
Graphics*, [Online]. Available: Telnet: database.carl.org Directory:
Other Information and Article Databases/Journal Graphics
File: long journey home

World Wide Web:

Collins, Stephen E. *Your Internet Kitchen*, [Online]. Available:
World Wide Web: http://web66.coled.umn.edu/ Directory:
Web66 Class room Internet Server Cookbook/Classroom
Internet Server Cook book File: Your Internet Kitchen

Notes

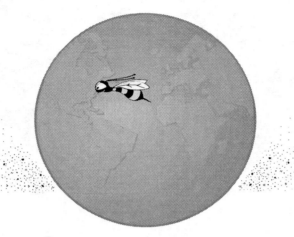

CHAPTER 7

Internet
Resources

Internet Resources

There are thousands of exit ramps to millions of pieces of information on the Internet. As an educator, parent, or student in K-12, you want to be able to explore the country roads and byways that will help you teach and learn. Road maps to these scenic areas will help you plan your journey down the information superhighway. These resources, project ideas, and lesson plans are not an exhaustive list, but will help you begin your adventure into the world of information access. Also note that the Internet is in flux. What you see today, you might not see tomorrow. Addresses and menu screens can change.

In order to find out what's new on the Internet, there are several publications you can read to keep you up-to-date. Here are some examples:

INFOBITS

INFOBITS is an electronic service of the Institute for Academic Technology's Information Resources Group. Each month they select material from information and technology sources and provide brief annotations in their publication.

To subscribe to INFOBITS, send e-mail to listserv@unc.edu with the following message:

SUBSCRIBE INFOBITS your_firstname your_lastname

Example: SUBSCRIBE INFOBITS Jane Doe

INFOBITS is also available online from The University of Washington's Gopher server.

gopher ike.engr.washington.edu

Academic Technology Services/
    Institute for Academic Technology/
        Infobits

Net-Happenings

Net-Happenings is a news group moderated by Gleason Sackman. The postings include announcements of new services, newsletters, conferences, and Internet tools. You can access it through your Usenet news reader or subscribe via e-mail.

To subscribe to Net-Happenings, send an e-mail to listserv@is.internic.net with the following message:

subscribe net-happenings your name

Example: subscribe net-happenings Jane Doe

The archives are available from MIDnet.

URL: http://www.mid.net/net/

gopher gopher.mid.net

Midnet's Catalog of Information Resources/
    Net-Happenings Listserv Archive

The Scout Report

InterNIC publishes a weekly newsletter to highlight new resources and other Internet news. The primary audience is the research and education community.

To subscribe to The Scout Report, send an e-mail message to majordomo@dsmail.internic.net with the following message:

subscribe scout-report

To access the hypertext version of the Report:

URL: http://rs.internic.net/scout_report_index.html

World Link Newsletter

World Link is a monthly newsletter targeted to the K-12 community for finding curriculum resources on the Internet. Pointers to lesson plans, announcements of projects, and tips for using the Internet in the classroom are a few of the subjects covered in each issue.

You can retrieve the text version from The Greater Columbus Free-net or AskERIC. You can also view the home page with direct links to places mentioned in the newsletter.

Home Page:

URL: http://www.smartpages.com/worldlink/worldlink.html

The Greater Columbus Freenet:

gopher gopher.freenet.columbus.oh.us

World Wide Gophers/North America/USA/Ohio/Greater Columbus Freenet/Education Center/Columbus Public Schools/ Dept. Library Media Services/World Link Newsletter

AskERIC:

gopher ericir.syr.edu

Electronic Journals, Books, and Reference Tools/
    Electronic Journals/
        World Link Newsletter

ARMADILLO

This is truly an innovative venture by the Houston School District. It was designed to support Texas history teachers by using an interdisciplinary method of teaching. Collaboration, multimedia, and accessing the Internet are used to teach history to middle school students. This gopher, as the readme text states, will not be static. Educators should explore this network to see how it might apply to their curriculum.

URL: gopher://riceinfo.rice.edu:1170/1

gopher riceinfo.ricr.edu
choose Other Gopher and Information Resources
choose Armadillo

Gopher Path:

World Wide Gophers/
  North America/
    USA/
      Texas/
        Armadillo

```
              Armadillo, the Texas Studies Gopher

   1.  About Armadillo (The Texas Studies Gopher from HISD)
   2.  More About Armadillo and Other Gophers/
   3.  Fact and Fiction About Armadillos/
   4.  Developmental History of Texas Studies Project/
   5.  Human Resource Development Opportunities/
   6.  Library Services and Resources/
   7.  Other Gophers and Information Servers with a Texas Twist/
   8.  Super Projects!!!/
   9.  Technology Help and Multimedia Software and Lessons  /
   10. **Texas Studies Instructional Information and Resources** /
   11. Weather Information/
   12. What's Happening/
   13. Search Armadillo by Title (Jughead)/
   14. Work in Progress/
```

ART AND IMAGES, TEXAS TECH

This site points to pictures from such places as the California Museum of Photography, the LBJ Library Collection, and Hubble Telescope. There is a menu item that allows you to search by keyword for images in all of Gopherspace.

URL: gopher://cs4sun.cs.ttu.edu:70/11/Art%20and%20Images

gopher cs4sun.cs.ttu.edu

Gopher Path:

World Wide Gophers/
  North America/
    USA/
      Texas/
        Texas Tech University, Computer Sciences/Art and Images

```
             Art and Images, Texas Tech University

     1.  ASCII Clipart Collection/
     2.  DOS and Mac viewing software/
     3.  TAEX Clip Art Collection (TIFF)/
     4.  U.S. Weather Map <Picture>
     5.  Entertainment Images from Texas A&M (GIF)/
     6.  Entertainment Images from U Michigan (GIF)/
     7.  WUARCHIVE Collection (GIF)/
     8.  WUARCHIVE Collection (JPEG)/
     9.  - - - - - - - - - - - - - - - - -
     10. Search for Pictures/Images in all of GopherSpace <?>
     11. - - - - - - - - - - - - - - - - -
     12. Animals, Plants, Scenic Beauty from U of Indiana/
     13. ArchiGopher: Images from U of Michigan/
     14. Architectural Projects from Johns Hopkins U/
     15. Art Gallery (from University of Vermont)/
     16. Astronomical Images (from U of Arizona)/
     17. Astronomical Images (from U of California at Irvine)/
```

18. Bicycling Pictures (from U of California, Irvine)/
19. Birds from U.S. Army/
20. Birds from U.S. Army (Individual descriptions)/
21. Bodleian Libraries Images (from Radcliffe Science Library)/
22. California Museum of Photography/
23. Campus Images from Michigan State University/
24. Campus Images from Texas A&M/
25. Campus Images from U of Texas at Austin/
26. Central American Images/
27. Centre for Innovative Computer Applications (Indiana Univ.)/
28. Craigdarroch Castle Images (from Victoria Freenet)/
29. Dallas Museum of Art - Information & Images/
30. Doctor Fun: The first daily cartoon of the Internet/
31. Endoscopic Test Images/
32. Global Satellite Images from NOAA and AMRC (collected by SSEC)/
33. Hubble Telescope Images/
34. Image Archives from NASA/
35. Imagenes Antiguas Culturas (Mexico)/
36. Imagenes Arquitectonicas (Mexico)/
37. Images from the LBJ Library Photo Collection/
38. Images of Hurricane Emily/
39. Images of Mars/
40. Images of the Earth/
41. Impressionist Art from U of Vermont/
42. Jackets and Photos Images (from MIT Univ. Press)/
43. Jewish Graphics (from Jerusalem One Network)/
44. Kandinsky Image Archive (from U.Mich Library)/
45. Kodak PhotoCD Images (via Johns Hopkins Univ.)/
46. Lunar Architecture (from U.Mich Library)/
47. MPEG Movies (from Texas A&M)/
48. MPEG Movies (from U of Texas)/
49. Maps and Images from Ann Arbor (from U.Mich Library)/
50. Music Images from U Wisconsin-Parkside/
51. NASA Ames GMS vis/IR images/
52. Nature and Science Pictures from Smithsonian/
53. PET Centre Medical Image Library (from Austin Hospital)/
54. Picasso in Mexico/
55. Pictures from Victoria Freenet/
56. Plant Species Images from Harvard U/
57. Postcard Collection from U of Vermont/

58. Russian Far East, Maps/
59. Soviet Archive Exhibit at Library of Congress/
60. Strange Interactions: Art Work by John E. Jacobsen/
61. Train Pictures (from plaza.aarnet.edu.au)/
62. U.S. Color Relief Maps/
63. Vatican Library Exhibit at Library of Congress/
64. Weather Images (University of Illinois)/
65. Weather Maps and Images (from Unidata)/
66. White House Pictures from Univ. of N. Carolina SUNsite/
67. White Shark Images from UC Berkeley/
68. Wolf Images and Sounds/
69. World Maps (DOS)/

AskERIC

AskERIC is a teacher's best friend. It is a service where a question can be asked on an educational topic and an answer is e-mailed to the individual. Lesson plans, clearinghouse documents, and archives of educational listservs are just a few of the many resources available from this system. AskERIC at: askeric@eicir.syr.edu

URL: gopher://ericir.syr.edu:70/11/

gopher ericir.syr.edu

Gopher Path:

World Wide Gophers/
   North America/
      USA/
         General/
            AskERIC

```
                    AskERIC Electronic Library
     1.  News and Information about ERIC and AskERIC/
     2.  Map of the Library/
     3.  Search AskERIC Menu Items <?>
     4.  AskERIC Toolbox (under construction)/
     5.  Frequently Asked Questions (FAQ's)/
     6.  AskERIC InfoGuides/
     7.  Lesson Plans/
     8.  Education Listservs Archives/
     9.  ERIC Clearinghouses/Components/
     10. ERIC Digests File/
     11. ERIC Bibliographic Database (RIE and CIJE)/
     12. Bibliographies/
     13. News & Announcements: Professional & Commercial Organizations/
     14. Other Education Resources/
     15. Education Conferences (Calendars and Announcements)/
     16. Electronic Journals, Books, and Reference Tools/
     17. Internet Guides and Directories/
     18. Gophers and Library Catalogs/
```

BBN'S

The national experimental network for schools contains curriculum resources, lesson plans, pointers to other gophers, and software.

URL: gopher://copernicus.bbn.com:70/11

gopher copernicus.nnb.com

Gopher Path:

World Wide Gophers/
  North America/
    USA/
      General/
        BBN'S

```
            BBN's National School Network Testbed

1.  Welcome to BBN's National School Network Testbed
2.  BBN Internet Server
3.  National School Network Testbed
4.  BBN - Educational Technologies Dept.
5.  K-12 on the Internet
6.  Software libraries
7.  AskERIC
8.  General information resources
9.  Internet information
10. State resources
11. Federal resources
12. Other Gopher and Information Servers
13. Search titles in gopherspace using Veronica


            National School Network Testbed

1.  About BBN's National School Network Testbed
2.  About BBN's National School Network Testbed (formatted - ..
3.  BBN Internet Server
4.  Getting the NII to School (text version)
5.  Testbed Conference April '93
6.  Ralph Bunche School, New York City
7.  San Diego City Schools
8.  Shadows Science Project
9.  UCSD InternNet Lesson Plans
10. California Dept. of Education - Sacramento
11. Co-NECT Project (NASDC)
12. MUSEs (Multi-user Simulation Environments) in education
```

BEST OF K-12 - TIESNET OF MINNESOTA

Tiesnet is one of the best places to search for examples of real world school projects. Wolf Study, Project Central America, and Circumpolar Expedition are a few of the many posted. There are lesson plans, pictures, and sounds to use with the projects. Many of these are still adaptable even if the project has been completed. It is a wonderful demonstration of interactivity among students, teachers, and other professionals involved in the projects.

URL: gopher://informns.k12.mn.us:70/11/best-k12

gopher informns.k12.mn.us

Gopher Path:

World Wide Gophers/
   North America/
     USA/
       Minnesota/
         K-12 Gophers/
         Best of K-12

```
                Best of K-12 Internet Resources (TIES)
     1.  Armadillo,Texas environmental, natural and cultural history and/
     2.  Bosnian/Croatian Exchange Project/
     3.  CNN newsroom classroom guide/
     4.  Canada's SchoolNet/
     5.  Children, Youth, and Family Consortium Clearinghouse/
     6.  Chukotka & Kamchatka [Russian Far East Exchange]/
     7.  Current K-12 Information (postings from Selected Ed Listservs)/
     8.  Daily Report Card News Service/
     9.  Dallas Museum of Art - Information & Images/
     10. Dictionary (Webster Server) <?>
     11. ENVIROnet (login:ENVIROnet, Password:henniker) <TEL>
     12. Education Gopher at Florida Tech/
     13. Electronic Books from Project Gutenberg/
     14. EnviroLink Network/
     15. Freenet Systems (Source of Academy 1)/
```

16. Geographic Server <TEL>
17. Great Lakes Information Network/
18. JOURNEY NORTH: Spring Migration 1995/
19. K12net/
20. KIDLINK Gopher/
21. MAYAQUEST/
22. Map the Monarchs!/
23. NASA/
24. NATIONAL PUBLIC TELECOMPUTING NETWORK(NPTN): Academy One/
25. National Education BBS(NEBBS) & Supercomputer(NESP) Login:new <TEL>
26. Newton Educational BBS (Login as cocotext) <TEL>
27. Project Central America/
28. Reports from McMurdo Station, Antarctica/
29. SELECTED PICTURES,QUICKTIME MOVIES & SOUNDS/
30. Search All White House Information for ... <?>
31. Selected Math and Science Resources
32. StarkNet (Stark County School District, Canton, Ohio, USA)/
33. TEACHER*PAGES (Pennsylvania Department of Education) Login:TX <TEL>
34. THE CIRCUMPOLAR EXPEDITION: May 11-18, 1994/
35. TIES Activities and Workshop Catalog/
36. Teacher Contacts/
37. The Internet Hunt/
38. The Ralph Bunche School ("The world's first elementary school/
39. The Space Science and Engineering Center (Global Satellite Images)/
40. TogetherNet, Foundation For Global Unity/
41. WOLF STUDY PROJECT/
42. Weather Information & Satellite Data and Images/
43. White House Information/
44. World School for Adventure Learning: The Journey North program/

BLUE SKIES

Blue-Skies is a specialized gopher display system written by Alan Steremberg, a University of Michigan student. It is sponsored by a grant from the National Science Foundation. With this program you can access and view hundreds of weather and environmental images, see animations of weather imaging taken within the last 24 hour period, and check the current forecast. In order to use the Blue-Skies program, you must download the software, be running TCP/IP, SLIP or PPP on a Macintosh computer. A program is being developed for Windows.

URL: gopher://groundhog.sprl.umich.edu:70/11/

Use Turbogopher to connect and retrieve the program.

gopher groundhog.sprl.umich.edu in software/Blue-Skies_1.0.sea.hqx

```
                    Blue Skies Gopher
1.   ~~~~~~~~~~~~~~~~~~~~~~~~~~~~~~~~~~~~~~~~~~~~~~~~~~~~~~
2.   | Blue-Skies INTERACTIVE images require our Mac |
3.   | gopher client to view them.  See the Software |
4.   | directory, it's easy to install!              |
5.   ~~~~~~~~~~~~~~~~~~~~~~~~~~~~~~~~~~~~~~~~~~~~~~~~~~~~~~
6.   :Blue-Skies_Home_Page.rof <Picture>
7.   :Help_and_Information/
8.   Air_Pollution/
9.   Current_Version=1.1
10.  Curriculum_Materials/
11.  Developers_Den/
12.  Exploring_the_Internet/
13.  Famous_Weather_Events/
14.  Interactive_Weather_Maps/
15.  International_Weather_Maps/
16.  International_Weather_Watchers/
17.  K-12 School Weather Observations <TEL>
18.  Ozone_Hole/
19.  Shoemaker-Levy Comet Images/
20.  Software/
21.  UM Weather <TEL>
22.  Weather_Animations/
```

CANADA'S SCHOOLNET GOPHER

SchoolNet is an educational networking initiative of Industry and Science Canada. Anyone with Internet access is free to use SchoolNet. Schools are asked to register so they will be able to make use of all the resources available. SchoolNet provides areas for discussion and information access in both French and English.

URL: gopher://gopher.schoolnet.carleton.ca:70/1

gopher gopher.schoolnet.carleton.ca

Gopher Path:

> World Wide Gophers/
> > North America/
> > > Canada/
> > > > Schoolnet

```
                    Canada's SchoolNet Gopher
  1.              Bienvenue au Reseau scolaire canadien/
  2.                  Welcome to SchoolNet                    /
  3.                                                          /
  4.  * * * * * * * * * * * * * * * * * * * * * * * * * * * */
  5.  SchoolNet Gopher/
  6.  Reseau scolaire canadien/
  7.  * * * * * * * * * * * * * * * * * * * * * * * * * * * */
  8.
  9.  SchoolNet MOO - Le MOO du RSC/
 10.  SchoolNet CHAT - CHAT du RSC/
 11.  SchoolNet WWW - WWW du RSC
 12.  SchoolNet FTP site - Site FTP du RSC/
 13.  Access to Newsgroups - Acceder aux babillards/
 14.  SchoolNet Listserver - Serveur de liste SchoolNet/
 15.  List of SchoolNet listservers
 16.  Tip of the Week - Conseil de la semaine/
 17.  SchoolNet Advisory Board Information/
```

CARL

Information databases such as Journal Graphics and the Librarian's Yellow Pages can be accessed and serached at CARL. Some of the the other resources on this network are restricted. This is a great source for Journal Graphics materials and the Librarian's Yellow Pages.

URL: telnet://pac.carl.org@CARL:23

telnet carl.pac.org login: PAC

Gopher Path:

World Wide Gophers/
  North America/
   USA/
    General/
     Consortium for School Networking/
      Resources on the Network/
       Resources for Education/
        CARL

```
CARL Corporation offers access to the followinggroups of databases:

        1. Library Catalogs
               (including Government Publications)

        2. Current Article Indexes and Access
               (including UnCover and ERIC)

        3. Information Databases
               (including Encyclopedia)

        4. Other Library Systems

        5. Library and System News

  Enter the NUMBER of your choice, and press the <RETURN> key >>
```

Children's Literature

New Mexico State University Library has a specific area devoted to children's literature. This server provides articles, book reviews, bibliographies, pointers to electronic books via Project Gutenberg, and other information.

URL: gopher://lib.nmsu.edu:70/11/.subjects/Education/.childlit

gopher lib.nmsu.edu

Gopher Path:

World Wide Gophers/
　　North America/
　　　　USA/
　　　　　　New Mexico/
　　　　　　　　New Mexico State University/
　　　　　　　　　　Library/
　　　　　　　　　　　　Resources by Subject/
　　　　　　　　　　　　　　Education/
　　　　　　　　　　　　　　　　Children's Literature

```
            Children's Literature - Electronic Resources
    1.  About Children's Literature: Electronic Resources
    2.  Announcements
    3.  Author Information
    4.  Awards
    5.  Bibliographies, Indexes & Library Guides
    6.  Calls for Papers
    7.  Children's Literature Centers & Collections
    8.  Conferences
    9.  Electronic Children's Books
    10. Electronic Journals & Book Reviews
    11. Internet Resources for Children's Literature
    12. Organizations
    13. Papers, Booktalks, Reader's Theater
    14. Professional Journals
    15. Publishers and Bookstores
    16. Syllabi
```

CICNET

The CICNet gopher is a collection of selected Internet resources of interest to K-12 educators, administrators, and students. It was designed by Jeanne Baugh, a professor of computer science at West Virginia University. One of the best features of this gopher is "Internet in the Classroom," which lists project resources including the Internet address, login and logout procedures, and notes about particularly useful files. There are also links to many menu choices.

URL: gopher://gopher.cic.net:3005/1

gopher gopher.cic.net 3005

Gopher Path:

World Wide Gophers/
  North America/
    USA/
      General/
        CICNet

```
                CICNet Select K-12 Internet Resources
    1.   About This Gopher
    2.   Search This Gopher (temporarily unavailable; sorry)
    3.   Gopher Servers/
    4.   World Wide Web Sites/
    5.   Telnet Sites/
    6.   FTP Sites/
    7.   Mailing Lists (listservs)/
    8.   Library Catalogs (list maintained by Yale University)/
    9.   Classroom Activities and Projects/
    10.  Publications/
    11.  Notices, News Flashes, and Other Short-term Information/
    12.  FYI (FAQs, training aids, and other resources)/
    13.  If You're Not Sure Where to Start
```

CoSN

The Consortium for School Networking is a membership organization of institutions formed to further the development and use of computer network technology in K-12 education. This gopher system is a gateway to hundreds of resources. It can be compared to a one-stop mega mall for educational resources. Examples of resources available via this gopher are CNN, Discovery Network, National Public Telecomputing Network, access to local and state networks, discussion groups, and information about educational projects and other service providers.

CoSN Membership
P.O. Box 8387
Berkeley, CA 94707-8387

URL: gopher://cosn.org:70/11/

gopher cosn.org

Gopher Path:

World Wide Gophers/
North America/
USA/
General/
Consortium for School Networking

Consortium for School Networking (COSN)

```
1.   About CoSN/
2.   Acknowledgments
3.   CoSN Gopher Welcomes You!/
4.   CoSN Logo/
5.   CoSN Information/
6.   CoSN Activities/
7.   Networking Information/
8.   Policy & Legislation/
9.   Resources on the Network/
10.  State and Local Network Projects/
11.  Educational Conferences/
12.  Related Organizations/
```

EISENHOWER NATIONAL CLEARINGHOUSE

The Clearinghouse is funded by the Eisenhower National Program for Mathematics and Science Education in the Office of Educational Research and Improvement (OERI), U.S. Department of Education.

A variety of resources are listed in the Clearinghouse catalog for teachers who want to construct lesson plans. Included in this gopher are pointers to curriculum materials in math and science.

Dial-up: 1-800-362-4448
Central Ohio: 292-9040

URL: gopher://enc.org:70/1

gopher enc.org

Gopher Path:

World Wide Gophers/
North America/
USA/
General/
Eisenhower National Clearinghouse

```
             Eisenhower National Clearinghouse
   1.   About this Gopher/
   2.   About ENC/
   3.   ENC Products and Services/
   4.   ENC Catalog of Curriculum Resources/
   5.   ENC & ERIC Resource Center/
   6.   Additional Curriculum Resources and Materials/
   7.   Reference Materials/
   8.   Curriculum Reform/
   9.   Testing and Assessment/
   10.  Promising Programs and Practices/
   11.  Professional Development Resources/
   12.  Federal Programs and Opportunities/
   13.  Educational Research/
   14.  News, Journals and Full Text/
   15.  Education, Math, Science Internet Sites/
   16.  Internet Software Tools/
```

EMPIRE SCHOOLHOUSE

The Empire Internet Schoolhouse is provided by the New York State Education and Research Network (NYSERNET) as part of their "bridging the gap program." Through this endeavor, collaboration and partnerships are fostered in the educational community by sharing resources and ideas. This will be a step toward meeting the needs of teachers and students at all levels. Empire Internet Schoolhouse provides a selection of K-12 resources, projects, and discussion groups from every corner of the Internet community.

URL: gopher://nysernet.org:3000/11/

telnet nysernet.org login: empire

Gopher Path:

World Wide Gophers/
  North America/
    USA/
      New york/
        New York State Education & Research.../
          School Collections K-12/
          Empire Internet Schoolhouse

```
          Empire Internet Schoolhouse (K-12)

1.   About the Empire Internet Schoolhouse
2.   Search Empire Gopher Titles and Menus <?>
3.   Assembly Hall for Projects and Discussions/
4.   Library & Internet Reference Tools/
5.   Academic Wings/
6.   School Reform and Technology Planning Center/
7.   Field trips to other school systems/
8.   Career and Guidance Office/
9.   Directory Services and Contacts Center/
10.  Electronic suggestion box (email to Empire's staff) <TEL>
11.  Special Collections: (The old k-12 directory)/
12.  The Grants Center/
```

FREE-NET CONNECTIONS

Gopher Path:

World Wide Gophers/
  North America/
    USA
      General/
        Consortium for Scool Networking/
        State and Local Network.../
          Freenets and Community Networks

Big Sky Telegraph - Dillon, Montana
  Internet: 192.231.192.1
  login: bbs

Buffalo Free-Net - Buffalo, New York
  Internet: freenet.buffalo.edu
  login: freeport

CapAccess - Washington, D.C.
  Internet: 128.164.140.32
  login: guest password: visitor

CIAO Free-Net - Trail, British Columbia, Canada
  Internet: 142.231.5.1
  login: guest

Cleveland Free-Net - Cleveland, Ohio
  Internet: freenet-in-a.cwru.edu
  login: Select #2 at first menu

Columbia Online Information Network (COIN) - Columbia, Missouri
  Internet: bigcat.missouri.edu
  login: guest

Dayton Free-Net - Dayton, Ohio
  Internet: 130.108.128.174
  login: visitor

Denver Free-Net - Denver, Colorado
  Internet: freenet.hsc.colorado.edu
  login: guest

Heartland Free-Net - Peoria, Illinois
 Internet: heartland.bradley.edu
 login: bbguest

Lorain County Free-Net - Elyria, Ohio
 Internet: freenet.lorain.oberlin.edu
 login: guest

National Capital Free-Net - Ottawa, Canada
 Internet: freenet.carleton.ca
 login: guest

Prarienet - Champaign-Urbana, Illinois
 Internet: prarienet.org
 login: visitor

Tallahassee Free-Net - Tallahassee, Florida
 Internet: freenet.fsu.edu
 login: visitor

Victoria Free-Net - Victoria, British Columbia, Canada
 Internet: freenet.victoria.bc.ca
 login: guest

Youngstown Free-Net - Youngstown, Ohio
 Internet: yfn.ysu.edu
 login: visitor

For Information on NPTN Contact:
National Public Telecomputing Network
P.O. Box 1987
Cleveland, Ohio 44106
Voice: 216-247-5800
FAX: 216-247-3328
e.mail: info@nptn.org
anonymous ftp site at: nptn.org
cd /pub/nptn/info.nptn)

GoMLINK, THE ELECTRONIC LIBRARY

GoMLink is a menu driven system that leads you to many resources, and is particularly strong in the K-12 area. CNN News lesson plans, AskERIC, and Free-nets are only a few of the many offerings that can be found by going through the menu screens.

URL: gopher://mlink.hh.lib.umich.edu:70/1

gopher mlink.hh.lib.umich.edu

Gopher Path:

World Wide Gophers/
  North America/
    USA/
      Michigan/
        Go-M-Link (Michigan)/
        Education

```
                  GoMLink, The Electronic Library
    1.   Search GoMLink's Menus  <?>
    2.   About Go M-Link/
    3.   Business & Economics/
    4.   Computers & Technology/
    5.   Education/
    6.   Entertainment & Recreation/
    7.   Environment/
    8.   Government, Politics & Law/
    9.   Health & Nutrition/
    10.  Humanities/
    11.  Libraries & Librarianship/
    12.  Michigan/
    13.  News Services, Newsletters & Journals/
    14.  Reference Desk/
    15.  Science/
    16.  Social Issues & Social Services/
    17.  The Internet & Its Other Resources/
```

GREATER COLUMBUS FREE-NET

    Free-nets are community based resource networks. You can view and retrive information posted by many different organizations such as city governments, libraries, and schools. The Greater Columbus Free-Net is an example of one of these community based bulletin boards.   The free-nets are set up in a manner similar to National Public Radio and Television. Registration is free, but they rely on community support and donations to continue operation.

URL: gopher://gopher.freenet.columbus.oh.us:70/1

gopher gizmo.freenet.columbus.oh.us

Gopher Path:

  World Wide Gophers/
    North America/
      USA/
        Ohio/
          Greater Columbus Free-Net

```
                    Greater Columbus Freenet
   1.  About the Greater Columbus Freenet (accounts, help, etc.)
   2.  How to find information on the FreeNet
   3.  Mail services
   4.  Discussion Groups
   5.  Account Management Functions
   6.  Social and Community Service Center
   7.  Business Center
   8.  Libraries and Information Resources
   9.  Health Services and Information
   10. Government Center
   11. Education Center
   12. News, Weather, Calendar
   13. Special Interest Groups
   14. Arts and Culture
   15. Other Internet Information Services
   16. What's New
```

INTERNIC: INTERNET NETWORK INFORMATION CENTER

Internic is a clearinghouse for locating information about the Internet. A searchable Directory of sites, publications, FAQs, and information about Internet culture are a few examples of the vast information you can find here.

URL: gopher://ds.internic.net.net:70/11/.ds

gopher ds.internic.net

Gopher Path:

World Wide Gophers/
  North America/
    USA/
      General/
        InterNIC: Internet Information Center

```
        InterNIC Directory and Database Services (AT&T)

    1.  About InterNIC Directory and Database Services/
    2.  InterNIC Directory of Directories/
    3.  InterNIC Directory Services ("White Pages")/
    4.  InterNIC Database Services (Public Databases)/
    5.  Additional Internet Resource Information/
    6.  Internet Documentation (RFC's, FYI's, etc.)/
    7.  National Science Foundation Information/
    8.  Search Anonymous FTP Site and Gopher Menu Indexes using Archie/
```

K-12 Gopher (Univ. of Massachusetts)

The K-12 server has a great main menu with links to areas that are often buried under many layers. The news services and reference links are especially helpful to students.

URL: gopher://k12.ucs.umass.edu:70/11/

gopher k12.ucs.umass.edu

Gopher Path:

World Wide Gophers/
  North America/
    USA/
      General/
        CICNet/
          Gopher Servers/
            K-12 Gopher (Univ. of Massachusetts)

```
                K-12 Gopher (Univ. of Massachusetts)

1.   About Gopher/
2.   Books, Dictionaries, Language Arts, Languages, Magazines, Thesauru../
3.   Conferences, Contests, Grants, Jobs, Workshops, Legislation/
4.   Educational Gophers, Policies/
5.   Entertainment (Fun and Games, MTV)/
6.   Five Colleges/Public School Partnership/
7.   Government, History, UN, Social Studies, Women's Studies/
8.   Images and Fine Arts/
9.   Internet Information, Policies; Gopher Jewels, Subject Guides/
10.  Libraries - UMass, Five Colleges, Massachusetts, and Others/
11.  News Services - Press reviews, newspapers/
12.  Other Gopher and Information Servers/
13.  Science, Agriculture, Ecology, Math, Space, Weather/
14.  Telecommunications Projects/
15.  UMass, Five Colleges, Amherst College Information/
16.  UMassK12, SpaceMet, Kidlink, and K12Net Informtion/
17.  4-H Energy Education Resources Database/
18.  Whois Services - Locate Internet EMail Addresses/
19.  What's New on UMassK12/
20.  basic/
```

K-12 Resources (NYSED)

This is one of the best K-12 resource gophers. Under each of the subject areas are pointers to materials. The Social Studies menu is very good, with pointers to historical documents.

URL: gopher://unix5.nysed.gov:70/11/k-12%20Resources

gopher unix5.nysed,gov

Gopher Path:

World Wide Gophers/
  North America/
    USA/
      General/
        CICNet/
          Gopher Servers/
            K-12 Resources (NYSED)

```
                    K-12 Resources (NYSED)
    1.   Arts & Humanities/
    2.   Disability Resources & Information/
    3.   English-Language Arts/
    4.   General/
    5.   Health, PhysEd & Home Ec/
    6.   Languages Other than English/
    7.   Math, Science & Technology/
    8.   Occupational and Technical/
    9.   Other Educational Gophers/
    10.  Social Studies/
    11.  Zip (Get There Faster)/
```

LC MARVEL

Bibliographic research guides, access to the Library of Congress Catalog, online exhibits, and a calendar of events are a few of the resources available on LC MARVEL. Especially interesting are the online exhibits which contain text and GIF image files about artifacts that have been on display at the Library of Congress. Currently available are 1492, African Mosaic, Dead Sea Scrolls, Russian Church and Native Alaskan Cultures, Soviet Archives, and Vatican. This is also the best place to find government information.

URL: gopher://marvel.loc.gov:70/1

gopher marvel.loc.gov

Gopher Path:

World Wide Gophers/
   North America/
      USA/
         Washington D C/
            Library of Congress (LC MARVEL)

```
                    Library of Congress (LC MARVEL)

  1.   About LC MARVEL/
  2.   Events, Facilities, Publications, and Services/
  3.   Research and Reference (Public Services)/
  4.   Libraries and Publishers (Technical Services)/
  5.   Copyright/
  6.   Library of Congress Online Systems/
  7.   Employee Information/
  8.   U.S. Congress/
  9.   Government Information/
  10.  Global Electronic Library (by Subject)/
  11.  Internet Resources/
  12.  What's New on LC MARVEL/
  13.  Search LC MARVEL Menus/
```

MURDOCK EDUCATIONAL MULTIMEDIA

As the name implies, this gopher server was designed for sharing multimedia files. Two examples are photographs from the Zaire exhibit and the 1994 Iditarod.

URL: gopher://davinci.vancouver.wsu.edu:70/1

gopher davinci.vancouver.wsu.edu

Gopher Path:

World Wide Gophers/
  North America/
    USA/
      General/
        Consortium for School Networking/
        Resources on the Network/
        Educational Resources/
          Murdock Educational Multimedia

```
              Murdock Educational Multimedia File Server
    1.   * HyperReport_README.
    2.   * Retrieving-HQX-Files.
    3.   * RetrievingTextFiles.
    4.   ** HR-Equip-Requirements.
    5.   Articles/
    6.   CompressionTools/
    7.   HR-Process-Samples/
    8.   HR-Tools&Instructions.sit <HQX>
    9.   Iditarod'94/
    10.  Interesting Gopher sites/
    11.  InternetInfo/
    12.  KidsStuff/
    13.  Site Index <?>
    14.  Site Index <?>
    15.  ZaireMuseum/
```

NASA SPACELINK

NASA Spacelink is a collection of NASA information and educational materials stored on a computer at the Marshall Space Flight Center in Huntsville, Alabama. Current space shuttle press kits, curriculum resources, and software programs can be found, as well as links to other NASA areas.

URL: http://spacelink.msfc.nasa.gov

gopher spacelink.msfc.nasa.gov

Gopher Path:

World Wide Gophers/North America/USA/General/
   CICNet/
     Gopher Sites/
      NASA SpaceLink

```
              Main Menu from: spacelink.msfc.nasa.gov
   1.   About.Spacelink/
   2.   Educational.Services/
   3.   Instructional.Materials/
   4.   NASA.News/
   5.   NASA.Overview/
   6.   NASA.Projects/
   7.   Spacelink.Frequently.Asked.Questions/
   8.   Spacelink.Hot.Topics/
```

NATIONAL PARENT INFORMATION NETWORK

The National Parent Information Network is now an information resource on the World Wide Web as well as onGopher. You can use any WWW browser (such as Mosaic, Cello, or Lynx) to view and download NPIN documents.

URL: http://www.prairienet.org/htmls/eric/npin/npinhome.html

gopher gopher.prairienet.org

Gopher Path:

World Wide Gophers/
   North America/
     USA/
       General/
         AskERIC/
           Other Education Resources/
           National Parent Information Network

```
                National Parent Information Network
    1.  NPIN Now Available on WWW
    2.  Welcome to the NATIONAL PARENT INFORMATION NETWORK
    3.  Parent News (updated weekly)/
    4.  Short Items Especially for Parents/
    5.  PARENTS AskERIC/
    6.  Ideas for Community Programs and Activities/
    7.  The Market Place/
    8.  Resources for Parent Educators/
    9.  ERIC Digests/
    10. ERIC Bibliographies/
    11. About NPIN and ERIC/
```

NEWTON

The U.S. Department of Energy's Argonne National Laboratory has a free nationwide bulletin board service for students and teachers. One of the main features of the service is "Ask a Scientist." Teachers or students can leave questions, which will be answered by scientists. Newton also has areas for sharing classroom ideas, a calendar of conferences, and E-Mail.

URL: telnet://cocotext@newton.dep.anl.gov:0

telnet newton.dep.anl.gov login: bbs

Gopher Path:

> World Wide Gophers/North America/USA/General/
> CICNet/
>> Telnet Sites/
>> Newton

```
             Welcome to Argonne National Laboratory's
                 Division of Educational Programs.

                     To login to the BBS,
                 PLEASE USE OUR NEW LOGIN OF
                           'bbs'

[[ Main Menu ]]
Argonne National Laboratory's NEWTON BBS

  Welcome To NEWTON!
  Check out our files section for teachers.  Dial-Up users can access
  files from the 3)Group 1)Files menu.  Internet users can access the
  same files via Anonymous FTP from newton.dep.anl.gov.  For more
  information, see the 3)Group 3)Discussion called XX)Sysop-System,
  6)HowTo and 8)WhatIsNew.


  The System Operator (sysop)

New Mail                                      Time left: 01 hr 16 min
1) System  2) Personal  3) Group  4) Network  5) SignOff  >
```

Northwest Ohio Computer Association K-12 Gopher Server

The Northwest Ohio Computer Association (NWOCA), a regional support agency of the Ohio Education Computer Network (OECN) designed their gopher for use by K-12 students; access is limited to resources deemed appropriate for minors. This server has one of the best reference sections for education. Along with a great search system for the CIA World Fact Book, it has the Geographic Name Server, and Local Times Around the World.

URL: gopher://nwoca7.nwoca.ohio.gov:70/1

gopher nwoca7.nwoca.ohio.gov

Gopher Path:

World Wide Gophers/
  North America/
    USA/
      Ohio/
        NWOCA\OECN K-12 Student Gopher Server

NWOCA\OECN K-12 Student Gopher Server

```
1.   About the OECN Gopher Server
2.   How to Obtain Changes to This Gopher Server
3.   Outline of This Gopher Server
4.   Government Center/
5.   Library Center/
6.   Local Time and Temperature (Toledo, Ohio USA)
7.   NW Ohio Alliance of Professional Development Providers (NWOAPDP)/
8.   NWOCA Electronic Mail Address Listing
9.   Ohio Department of Education (ODE) Resources/
10.  Other Information Resources/
11.  Reference Center/
12.  School House/
13.  Weather Center/
```

Other Information Resources

1. Airline Reservation Telephone Numbers
2. Airport 3-Letter Identification Codes
3. Almanac and Sports Schedule (U. Chicago)
4. American Chemical Society Books Catalog/
5. Amtrak Train Schedules (George Washington University)/
6. Automobile Rental Reservation Telephone Numbers
7. Calendars/
8. Entertainment - Top 10 Listings (CNS)/
9. Hotel Reservation Telephone Numbers
10. International Telephone Country/City Dialing Codes
11. Murphy's Laws & Related Materials
12. NFL Scores and Standings (Wicat Systems, Utah)
13. Network and Technical Resources/
14. Professional Sports Schedules (Colorado)/
15. Recipes (Wahington & Lee University)/
16. Recipes Database Search (Brown) <?>
17. Time (Local) Around the World/
18. Toll-free Phone Numbers for Computer Companies
19. Toll-free Phone Numbers for Non-Profit Organizations

PUBLIC BROADCASTING SERVICE (PBS)

The focus of this server is the dissemination of study guides, teachers's guides, licensing information, and other materials based on PBS programming schedules.

URL: gopher://gopher.pbs.org:70/11/

gopher gopher.pbs.org

Gopher Path:

> World Wide Gophers/
>> North America/
>>> USA/
>>>> General/
>>>>> Public Broadcasting Service (PBS) Gopher

```
                      Public Broadcasting Service
     1.  Welcome to the Public Broadcasting Service gopher server
     2.  About the PBS gopher server
     3.  Adult Learning Service (Telecourses)/
     4.  Adult Learning Satellite Service (ALSS)/
     5.  K-12 Learning Services/
     6.  NEW! National Program Service (NPS) program listings/
     7.  PBS MATHLINE/
     8.  PBS ONLINE/
     9.  PBS VIDEO/
     10. Press Releases/
     11. Other Gopher and Information Servers/
```

SCHOLASTIC INTERNET LIBRARY GOPHER

The Scholastic Internet Center is a sampling of the information available through membership in Scholastic Network. The system is periodically updated and contains curriculum materials with lesson plans.

URL: gopher://scholastic.com:2003/11/

gopher scholastic.com 2003

Gopher Path:

World Wide Gophers/
   North America/
      USA/
         Pennsylvania/
            Common Knowledge/
               K12 Education Resources/
                  Scholastic Internet Center

```
                Scholastic Internet Library Gopher
   1.   Welcome to Scholastic!
   2.   What's New/
   3.   The Ultimate Education Store/
   4.   Scholastic Internet Libraries/
   5.   Scholastic Electronic Publications/
   6.   Scholastic Network/
   7.   Scholastic Inc./
   8.   Scholastic Business Opportunities/
   9.   Feedback
   10.  Search/
```

Smithsonian Institution

The Smithsonian Institution offers a tremendous library of GIF images from their museum collections. GIF files were created by CompuServe to be read universally by all computers. Text files describing the photographs are available, and can be transferred using Anonymous FTP, then downloaded to your hard drive. Software for viewing the photographs can also be transferred and downloaded.

URL: ftp://photo1.si.edu/

ftp photo1.si.edu
    Image Path: /images/gif89a
    Text Path: /smithsonian.photo.info.txt

```
ftp> cd /images/gif89a
250 CWD command successful.
ftp> dir
200 PORT command successful.
150 Opening ASCII mode data connection for /bin/ls.
total 34
drwxr-xr-x   2 root      root         2048 Feb 24 19:38 air-space
drwxr-xr-x   2 root      root         1024 Feb 14 12:23 art
drwxr-xr-x   2 root      root         2048 Feb 24 19:38 new-photo-uploads
drwxr-xr-x   2 root      root         4096 Feb 14 15:19 people-places
drwxr-xr-x   2 root      root         3584 Feb 24 19:38 science-nature
drwxr-xr-x   2 root      root         3584 Feb 24 19:38 tech-history
226 Transfer complete.
414 bytes received in 0.035 seconds (12 Kbytes/s)
```

The Smithsonian also maintains a Natural History gopher system full of information about science.

URL: gopher://nmnhgoph.si.edu:70/1

gopher nmnhgoph.si.edu

Gopher Path:

World Wide Gophers/
  North America/
    USA/
      Washington D C/
        Smithsonian Institution's Natural History

Smithsonian Institution's Natural History Gopher

1. About the SI Natural History Gopher (& What's New)
2. Botany at the Smithsonian Institution/
3. Invertebrate Zoology at the Smithsonian Institution/
4. Paleontology at the Smithsonian Institution/
5. Vertebrate Zoology at the Smithsonian Institution/
6. Smithsonian Biodiversity Programs and Data/
7. Smithsonian Biological Conservation Programs and Data/
8. Smithsonian Global Volcanism Program/
9. Smithsonian Laboratory of Molecular Systematics/
10. Smithsonian Natural History Information and Announcements/
11. Museum Computerization and Technology/
12. Related Gopher and Information Servers/

Teacher Education Internet Server

The Teacher Education Internet Server was created by the University of Virginia and the University of Houston. It was established to explore ways in which the Internet can benefit teacher education programs around the world. Users can participate in discussions, download self-instructional modules, and access electronic versions of *Ed-Tech Review* and *Technology and Teacher Education Annual.*

URL: gopher://teach.virginia.edu:70/1

telnet state.virginia.edu login: gopher

Gopher Path:

>World Wide Gophers/
>>North America/
>>>USA/
>>>>Virginia/
>>>>>Teacher Education Internet Server

```
              Teacher Education Information Server (TEIS)

     1.  About the Teacher Education Internet Server/
     2.  Electronic_Publications/
     3.  Mathematics Education/
     4.  Research/
     5.  Reading and Language Arts/
     6.  Social Studies/
     7.  Special Education/
     8.  Educational Technology/
     9.  International Education/
     10. Soc. for Info. Technology and Teacher Ed. (SITE) Information/
     11. Teach-IT Modules/
     12. Software_Archives/
     13. Telecommunications and Networking/
     14. Interactive Resources <TEL>
     15. Other Internet Resources/
     16. Grants, Development Opportunities, Workshops/
```

U.S. Department of Education/ OERI Gopher Server

The U.S. Department of Education offers many valuable resources to teachers including grant information, publications, and educational software.

URL: gopher://gopher.ed.gov:70/1

gopher gopher.ed.gov

Gopher Path:

> World Wide Gophers/
> > North America/
> > > USA/
> > > > General/
> > > > > U.S. Department of Education

```
                    U.S. Department of Education

    1.   About This Gopher/
    2.   What's New in This Gopher/
    3.   Search this Gopher by Key Words (Jughead)/
    4.   U.S. Department of Education Programs-General Information/
    5.   Department-wide Initiatives (Goals 2000...)/
    6.   Educational Research, Improvement, and Statistics (OERI & NCES)/
    7.   Elementary and Secondary Education (OESE), and Early Childhood/
    8.   School-to-Work, Vocational and Adult Education (OVAE)/
    9.   Announcements, Bulletins, and Press Releases/
    10.  U.S. Department of Education/OERI Publications/
    11.  U.S. Department of Education Phone Directory <CSO>
    12.  Educational Software/
    13.  Other Education Gophers and VERONICA Searches/
```

U. S. <u>G</u>overnment

White House

To e-mail the president, send a message to

president@whitehouse.gov

To e-mail the vice-president, send a message to

vice-president@whitehouse.gov

You will receive a message stating your e-mail was received. To receive a response, you will need to include your postal address.

URL: http://www.whitehouse.gov

On the White House web server, you can listen to messages from the President and Vice-President, learn about the First Family, leave a message for the White House, and link to other government servers.

U.S. House Of Representatives - Home Page

U.S. House of Representatives
Home Page

Welcome to the U.S. House of Representatives' World Wide Web Service

The U.S. House of Representatives' World Wide Web service provides public access to legislative information as well as information about Members, Committees, and Organizations of the House and to other U.S. government information resources.

Congress

Information on bills, e-mail addresses, documents about the congressional process, status of bills, full text of bills, and committee schedules are just a few of the items located at House and Senate locations.

House of Representatives

gopher gopher.house.gov

URL: http://www.house.gov/

Senate

gopher gopher.senate.gov

URL: gopher://gopher.senate.gov:70/1

Thomas Legislative Information

This server contains full text legislation searchable by keyword or bill number. It also points to other government information.

URL: http://thomas.loc.gov/

Federal Agencies and Branches

The Library of Congress has a path to government branches and their agencies through its gopher system. It is the best one stop-source for this kind of information.

gopher marvel.loc.gov

Government Information/
  Federal Information Resources/
    Information by Branch of Government/

Way Cool World Wide Web

The World Wide Web offers a tremendous amount of information in the form of hypermedia — pictures, sound, animation, interactivity, and more.

Some good starting points for the beginner

KID (Kid's Internet Delight)

>   http://www.clark.net/pub/journalism/kid.html

>   This server is chock full of information for children — from an interactive story with Theodore Tugboat to an awesome space calendar listing events for the coming year.

The Children's Page

>   http://www.pd.astro.it/forms/dearlife.shtml

>   This host is Fun for the whole family. The Astronomical Observatory of Padova, Italy maintains this web site in both Italian and English. Here you can visit a wooden toy exhibit, learn about Italian history, visit the LEGO site in Norway, and even leave a message.

Kid's Web

>   http://www.npac.syr.edu/textbook/kidsweb/

>   Part of the Living Textbook Project, this site points to places by subject area. It has wonderful links to museums, science collections, geography, and other information.

Kids on Campus

http://www.tc.cornell.edu/Kids.on.Campus/KOC94/

You are welcomed with road signs of places from which to choose. Take Solar System Street to the Planet Earth where you will find comprehensive information about the sun and planets. The Daily Gazette takes you to a gopher menu of news resources while Ithaca 6 gives you local information. Choosing Dinosaurs will speed you off to the Museum of Paleontology and choosing Expo takes you to exhibits. Visit the Library and you will find reference information. If you are lost on the Internet, go to the Tourist Center for help in traveling the information highway.

List of individual web sites and a brief description of each:

Academy One

http://nptn.org/cyber.serv/AOneP/

Part of the National Public Telecomputing Network, Academy One is loaded with projects targeted to K-12.

ART-ROM Museum Web

http://www.primenet.com/art-rom/museumweb/

Art-ROM, Ltd. is a commercial organization involved in communications, and marketing museums and CD-ROM products. This server has links to places such as the Coyote Point Museum for Environmental Education, Tucson Museum of Art, and University of Wyoming Art Museum.

ARTSEDGE

http://k12.cnidr.org/janice-k12/artsedge/artsedge.html

Supported by the National Endowment for the Arts and the U.S. Department of Education, ARTSEDGE provides the Information Gallery, links to art education resources, and information about art in K-12 education.

ArtServe

http://rubens.anu.edu.au

Australian National University's gallery of art history presents a tremendous number of pictures of classical, medieval, and renaissance architecture and sculpture.

AskERIC Virtual Library

http://ericir.syr.edu

There is a slide show, satellite images, and a teachers guide from the NASA SIR-CED lessons, plus links to all kinds of educational resources on their gopher system.

Aurora Page

http://www.geo.mtu.edu/weather/aurora

Information and images are posted about the Northern Lights.

Carlos's Coloring Book

http://robot0.ge.uiuc.edu/~carlosp/color/

Choose between simple and expert modes. Pick from birthday, Christmas, crown, flower, house, or snowman pictures. Color them interactively and save them. This web is brought to you by Carlos A. Pero.

Carrie's Sites for Educators

http://www.mtjeff.com/~bodenst

Nice collection of links to educational sites.

Center for Mars Exploration

http://cmex-www.arc.nasa.gov/

Current news, pictures, and information about past, present, and future missions to Mars are available at the Center for Mars Exploration.

Children's Literature Web Guide

http://www.ucalgary.ca/~dkbrown/index.html

An amazing collection of materials related to children's literature can be found on this excellent web site. You will find book awards, subject bibliographies, information about authors, resources for teachers, parents, and storytellers, children's writings and ways for young people to contribute as well as links to many other places.

CIA Web Server

http://www.ic.gov/

The CIA web sever is a great place to find information about other countries through the *CIA World Factbook*. Along with information about places, there is a black and white outline map of each country, and regional color maps. There is also information about the CIA and the *Factbook on Intelligence*.

Cisco Educational Archive

http://sunsite.unc.edu/cisco/edu-arch.html

Under the Educational Catalog's Greatest Hits, you will find links to SpaceLINK, Frog Dissection, Froggy Page, Using Computer Networks in the K-12 Classroom Tutorial, and more.

City Net

http://www.city.net/

The most comprehensive area on the Internet about cities, including information on what to see and where to stay.

Civil War Letters from an Iowa Soldier

http://www.ucsc.edu/civil-war-letters/home.html

This site is a good source for original Civil War material. The Letters were written by Newton Robert Scott to Hannah Cone about his personal experiences during the Civil War. A librarian compiled this material from a family collection.

Concertina

http://www.digimark.net/iatech/books

Concertina is a Canadian children's publisher that has published online versions of some of their books. *Waking in Jerusalem* by Sharon Katz and *I live on a Raft* by Jerzy Harasymowicz are posted.

Currency Converter

http://gnn.com/cgi-bin/gnn/currency

This is a very nice interface for determining current exchange rates for currency. Just select the desired currency and all other currencies will be converted relative to the one you selected. It is updated weekly.

Cybrary of the Holocaust

http://www.best.com/~mddunn/cybrary

You will find links to many resources such as the Holocaust Museum and Jerusalem One. There are also journals of survivors, historical perspectives, and witness facts.

Daily Planet

http://www.atmos.uiuc.edu/

The Department of Atmospheric Sciences at the University of Illinois hosts this web of multimedia materials and instruction on meteorology.

Dr. Duey Neadums Wacky Web Page

http://scitech.lm.com/

A commercial company for science and technology products has created this interactive web page. The Discovery Science Trail, where a question is posed with a choice of answers, has a catch — you must send for the answer to the questions. They are not available online.

Dr. Fun

http://sunsite.unc.edu/Dave/drfun.html

Humorous cartoons created by Dave Farley are located here.

Earthquake - Current

file://garlock.wr.usgs.gov/pub/CURRENT/current.html

Black and white or color maps pinpointing current seismic activity are posted on this server.

Earthquake Information

http://info.er.usgs.gov/research/environment/hazards/
earthquake/earthquake-education.html

This site, hosted by the U.S. Geological Survey, has lots of pointers to information about earthquakes.

EdWeb

http://edweb.cnidr.org:90

EdWeb hosts information on educational reform and technology with links to other networks.

EINet Galaxy

http://www.einet.net/

The Galaxy is a guide to worldwide information and services and is provided as a public service by Einet. The information is organized by topic and can be searched. There are many links to science and math resources.

Eisenhower National Clearinghouse

http://www.enc.org

ENC is one of the best resources for locating math and science curriculum materials. You can search their catalog of resources or follow their links to other actovotoes and lesson plans.

Exploratorium ExploraNet

http://www.exploratorium.edu

The Exploratorium is a museum of science, technology, and human perception located in the Palace of Fine Arts in the Marina district of San Francisco. There are interactive digital versions of Exploratorium activities that students can use. You can also ask questions by filling out an online form; an Exploratorium staff member will contact you with an answer.

Expo

http://sunsite.unc.edu/expo/ticket_office.html

The Expo is a starting point for hypermedia exhibits on the Internet. It has pointers to the Spalato, Vatican, Paleontology, and more. Get your ticket and take a tour. Then reserve a table for six and relax in the cafe.

Faces of Science: African-Americans in the Sciences

http://www.lib.lsu/lib/chem/display/faces.html

A presentation prepared for Black History Month at Louisiana State University for 1995. The virtual exhibit is based on a poster series shown in the Chemistry library. Along with photographs are biographical descriptions, charts, and references of African-American contributions to science.

FedWorld

http://www.fedworld.gov/

Information found here is provided by many federal agencies.

Field Museum of Natural History

http://www.bvis.uic.edu/museum/

You won't want to miss a visit to this museum. It has two great exhibits: DNA to Dinosaurs and Javanese Mask Collection. In DNA to Dinosaurs, there are awesome pictures of these giants from the past as well as animations, sound, and 3-D.

Fire Safety

http://www.abag.ca.gov/abag/local_gov/city/san_carlos/fire/
firedept.html

The City of San Carlos, California, has provided a fire and safety
tutorial with emphasis on preventing wildland fires.

Franklin Institute Virtual Science Museum

http://sln.fi.edu

The doors are always open at this museum for viewing Benjamin
Franklin: Glimpses of the Man and The Heart: A Virtual Exploration.

French Ministry of Culture French Cave Paintings

http://www.culture.fr/gvpda.htm

This is a link on the French Ministry of Culture's home page that
leads to text and four images about the Combre d'Arc prehistoric
cave art discovery.

Frog Dissection

http://curry.edschool.virginia.edu/~insttech/frog

This is an online tutorial designed to be used with high school
biology students who are learning to dissect a frog. Photographs
are shown of students performing the dissection techniques on real
frogs.

Gallery of Interactive Online Geometry

http://www.geom.umn.edu/apps/gallery.html

Draw or explore with different geometry programs on this interactive server.

Games

http://www.bu.edu/Games/games.html

Tic Tac Toe, Pegs, and a multi-player game Hunt the Wumpus are provided by Boston University.

Godiva Chocolate Online

http://www.godiva.com/

Want to know the history of chocolate, find recipes, buy chocolate, or read articles from the *Chocalatier Magazine*? This is the place to go.

Grand Canyon National Park

http://www.kbt.com/gc/gc_home

Trail maps, trail descriptions, a historical timeline, other things to see in the area, photos, and books can be found on this nicely designed web server.

Guide to Covered Bridges

http://129.25.48.205/top/bridge1/CB1.HTML

You are greeted with Die Grosse Bruke uder den Schuylkill from a nineteenth century German print. There are FAQ sheets with pictures of covered bridges categorized by structural type, a driving tour, images by season, and bridges in other regions.

Hubble Telescope Pictures

http://www.stsci.edu/public.html

View pictures from the Hubble telescope.

Imaginary Exhibit - France

http://dmf.culture.fr

In this exhibition from eighteen museums, a collection of 100 artists provides a panorama of French culture during the eighteenth century. The text is written in French.

Internet College Exchange

http://www.usmall.com/college

ICX provides links to college and university home pages that supply varying degrees of information about their academic programs, tuition, and financial aid. You can search for a specific college by submitting a request on a web search form. There are also documents on choosing a college, how to select the ideal school, and sources for financial aid.

Internet Public Library

http://ipl.sils.umich.edu/

Select from a map of different locations in the library to explore.
The Youth Services section will take you to several choices such as
Ask the Author where you can submit questions and learn
information about the person. This is a great site you won't want
to miss.

James T. Kirk Sing-a-long Page

http://www.ama.caltech.edu/~mrm/kirk.html

Portions of songs recorded in 1968 by William Shatner are located
here. Selections include *Mr. Tambourine Man* and *Lucy in the Sky
with Diamonds* from the *Transformed Man* album.

Janice's K-12 OUTPOST

http://k12.cnidr.org/janice_k12/k12menu.html

Are you looking for new places and projects on the Internet? The
OUTPOST has a nice collection from which to choose.

Jerusalem Mosaic

http://shum.cc.huji.ac.il/jeru/jerusalem.html

The Jerusalem Mosaic contains information, exhibits, and pictures
about the city.

K-12 Internet Sites

http://toons.cc.ndsu.nodak.edu/~sackman/k12.html

Current K-12 web sites are listed with direct links to them.

Le Weblouvre

http://sunsite.unc.edu/louvre/

Take a tour of the Louvre or Paris on this web server. Voted one of the best for 1994.

Library of Congress

http://lcweb.loc.gov/homepage/lchp.html

The Library of Congress is home to several exhibits from their special collections. Of particular interest is the American Memory Project which has the following: Early Motion pictures from the Library of Congress, 1897-1916; Selected Civil War photographs from the Library of Congress, 1861-1865; Color Photographs from the Farm Security Administration/Office of War Information, ca. 1938-1944; and Documents from the Folklore Project, Federal Writers' Project, 1936-1940. In addition, there are online exhibits — African American Mosaic, 1492, the Vatican, Soviet Archives, and the Dead Sea Scrolls.

MegaMath

http://www.c3.lanl.gov/mega-math/welcome.html

MegaMath has a wonderful collection of math resources designed for the elementary level. Included are lesson plans and activities.

MidLink Magazine

http://longwood.cs.ucf.edu:80/~MidLink/

Here is a terrific place for students 10 to 15 to participate in an electronic magazine. Any school is welcome to participate by submitting material via snail mail or FTP. Visit the site for more details.

Museum of Paleontology

http:ucmp1.berkeley.edu/welcome.html

Also known as the "Hall of Dinosaurs," you can visit several areas including the Dilophosaur Exhibit narrated by the discoverer, Sam Welles, Professor Emeritus.

NASA Global Quest

http://quest.arc.nasa.gov

This web server is the home of The Internet in the Classroom. There are frequently asked questions (FAQ), Getting Us Teachers Online, and interactive projects.

NASA Historic Archives

http://www.ksu.nasa.gou/history/history.html

Historical photographs and information about the space program are provided.

NASA Home Page

http://www.gsfc.nasa.gov/NASA_homepage.html

There are many links to other NASA servers on this home page.

NASA Online Educational Resources

http://www.gfc.nasa.gov/nasa_online_education.html

This is a collection of Internet sources at NASA and affiliated organizations. Included is a catalog of NASA earth and science CD-ROMs, information about the Jason Project, and NASA hot topics.

NASA SPACELINK

http://spacelink.msfc.nasa.gov/

SpaceLINK offers a hypermedia version of its popular text based server, with lots of curriculum resources from lesson plans to current information about the space program.

Natural History Museum in Berne, Switzerland

http://www-nmbe.unibe.ch/index.html

Are you a dog lover? Do you like Saint Bernards? If the answer is yes, you won't want to miss this site. The museum provides history and information on seven Swiss breeds and a separate article on the Saint Bernard.

Northern Lights Planetarium

http://www.uit.no/npt/homepage-npt.en.html

This is an exhibit from Norway with information about Aurora Borealis from both a scientific and human perspective.

Odyssey of the Mind

http://www.odyssey.org/odyssey

This organization sponsors team-based problem solving activities for students. Included is information on how to join.

Pathfinder from Time Warner

http://www.timeinc.com

An array of information is provided by Time Warner from their vast resources. There are full text articles from *Time*, *Vibe*, and *Entertainment Weekly*. They also have a "Virtual Garden," which has a searchable index to the *Gardening Encyclopedia*.

Planetary Society

http://wea.mankato.mn.us/TPS/

The Planetary Society was founded by Carl Sagan and Bruce Murray. Their online exhibit has links to a collection of information on planets and a search for extraterrestrial life.

Plugged In

http://www.pluggedin.org/

This non-profit group is dedicated to bringing educational opportunities created by new technologies to children and families from low-income communities.

Ralph Bunche School

http://Mac94.ralphbunche.rbs.edu/

gopher ralphbunche.rbs.edu

Based in Harlem, this is a great example of a testbed site where students are learning to be information providers.

Sea World/Busch Gardens

http://www.bev.net/education/SeaWorld/homepage.htlm

This is an information database that provides elementary level teacher's guides for the study of marine animals.

Scholastic Center

http://www.scholastic.com

Press Return, a multimedia magazine written by students with editorial assistance by the staffers at Scholastic, is the highlight on this web server. Those schools who subscribe to Scholastic Network are involved in the project. There are also pointers to other educational resources and the Scholastic Gopher.

Shoemaker Levy 9 Collision with Jupiter Impact Home Page

http://seds.lpl.arizona.edu/sl9/sl9.html

You will find spectacular pictures, animations, and other resources regarding the collision of fragments of comet P/Shoemaker-Levy 9 with Jupiter, which took place on July 16—22, 1994.

Smithsonian

http://www.si.edu/

This is a gateway to many of the servers from the Smithsonian, including the National Air & Space Museum, Natural History Web, and the Photo Server of images from the museum collections.

Space Calendar

http://newproducts.jpl.nasa.gov/calendar

Included are space-related activities and anniversaries for the coming year. Launch dates are subject to change. Anniversary dates are listed in five-year increments. There are links to pictures and text about the event. This is a spectacular server.

Star Trek Generations

http://generations.viacom.com/

Paramount and Viacom developed this site to promote the motion picture *Star Trek Generations*. There are pictures, sounds, movie previews, and other information.

Street Cents Online

http://www.screen.com/streetcents.html

Consumer information for students is available at this site.

Theodore Tugboat's Online Activity Center

http://www.screen.com

Participate in an interactive story with Theodore Tugboat by choosing what he should do next, review a synopsis of episodes, find descriptions of characters, download a page from the online coloring book, or share ideas via e-mail.

United States Holocaust Museum

http://www.ushmm.org/

Information is available about museum visits, programs, and its education area. You will also find a brief history, teaching guidelines, FAQs, an article on children of the Holocaust, and an annotated videography.

Virology

http:/bocklabs.wisc.edu/Welcome.html

View pictures of microscopic viruses and learn information about them.

VolcanoWorld

http://volcano.und.nodak.edu/

This a great web site for all kinds of resources related to volcanoes. It is designed for school children and visitors at Hawaii Volcanoes National Park and Mt. St. Helen's Monument. They have reports and pictures of the latest eruptions, photos of many other volcanoes, an Ask the Volcanologist section, lesson plans, and even a volcano mall.

Volcanoes

http://www.geo.mtu.edu/volcanoes/

Information and pictures about Mount St. Helen's and Mount Pinatubo are found at this site.

Web66

http://web66.coled.umn.edu/

Web66 is a wonderful resource for teachers and students who want to create their own web sites with a Macintosh computer. You can find a step-by-step guide and HTML pages to download.

Weather Browser (Interactive)

http://rs560.cl.msu.edu/weather/interactive.html

Type in the three letter station code such as CMH for Columbus, Ohio, or click on the map and you will receive a report of current weather conditions.

WebMind

http://einstein.et.tudelf.nl/~mudlaan/WebMind/WM_intro.html

This is a web version of the popular educational game, MasterMind.

Welcome to the Planets

http://stardust.jpl.nasa.gov/planets/

Welcome to the Planets contains planet profiles, pictures, and descriptions of the space vehicles that were used in their exploration. This is a good resource for students interested in this topic.

World Maps

http://pubweb.parc.xerox.com/map

This is a Gazetteer along with world maps. Type in the name of a city, and its location by latitude and longitude will be returned.

Yahoo

http://www.yahoo.com

This is one of the most comprehensive directories of information found on the World Wide Web.

CHAPTER 8

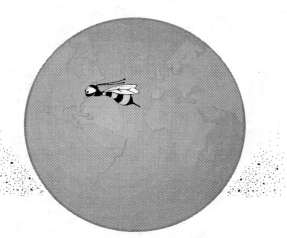

Project
Ideas

INTERNET PROJECT IDEAS

This section is compiled from files available on the Internet. There are several resources which will help teachers and students to find projects and interact with other classrooms across the country and around the world. Good starting points are the *Internet Resource Directory Part IV: Infusion Ideas* by Judi Harris and *How Teachers Find Projects* compiled by Beverly Hunter. Both are available on the Internet. Many of the Infusion Ideas are listed as individual menu items on the CICNet gopher along with *How Teachers Find Projects*. Armadillo, K12Net, the National Public Telecomputing Network's Academy One, and KIDLINK are other areas where you can find and participate in projects. Listservs are another good source.

If you are interested in starting a project, read *Keys to Successful Projects* from Global SchoolNet. It has helpful information on how to design a project and a template for participation. Gopher cosn.org and follow this path to the text file: Resources on the Network/Network Resources for Education/ Telecommunications Projects/Keys to Successful Projects.

Academy One

Included are curriculum-based projects that teachers have developed for use with their students. They encourage all levels of computer users to participate. By recognizing the many different learning styles, projects remain flexible for sharing information and creating the classroom without walls. The following are examples of projects from Academy One. The complete list can be found on the National Public Telecomputing Network: ftp nptn.org in /pub/nptn/info.nptn.

URL: http://nptn.org/cyber.serv/AOneP/

The Academy One FAQ sheet states these four ways for participating: (1) dialing directly to one of the NPTN affiliates; (2) telnet to an NPTN affiliate; (3) send/receive e-mail; or (4) place Academy One on your server.

You can obtain a list of the NPTN affiliates in the following ways (1) via Anonymous FTP ftp.nptn.org in /pub/nptn/nptn.info; (2) telnet to nptn.org; login as visitor and look through the Administration Building; or (3) send an e-mail request to info@nptn.org.

Sample Projects

NESPUT TELEOLYMPICS - A "Virtual" Olympics
(Grades 1-12; March to May)

Students compete in a series of track events in their own schoolyards, posting the winning scores in each category to the computer network. Results are compared, and international winners receive recognition. In addition to the track events, Opening and Closing ceremonies are conducted like the real Olympics, and information is exchanged about schools and communities around the world.

FOREST DAY -
[Multiple grade levels; Special Event - September 24, 1993]

This will be a day to reflect on the importance of the forest. This activity includes discussions on the various types, from rain forests to kelp forests. Activities include a school-site tree inventory, forest picture (GIF file) exchange, and analysis of the effect of deforestation on the earth's climate using the Lawrence Livermore supercomputer center.

STRUCTURES; TECHNOLOGY AND SCIENCE FOR YOUNG CHILDREN - [Ages 5-8; On-going project]

This project contains thirteen problem-solving and learning activities that use literature to integrate technology and science instruction across the elementary curriculum for early childhood. A moderated discussion area with the grant-winning mentor teacher will continue throughout the school year.
Contact: Cathy Ney (cney@radford.vak12ed.edu)

LA CLASSE GLOBALE FRANCOPHONE (La CGF) -
[Multiple grade levels; On-going project]

This is an electronic classroom designed for communications in French between young people of all ages and all countries. The area will include the news from France in French five days a week and moderated discussions with lesson plans that change regularly.
Contact: Yona Webb (aa844@cleveland.freenet.edu)

NPTN STUDENT NEWS NETWORK -
[Multiple grade levels; On-going project]

Schools are encouraged to contribute electronic editions of their school newspapers. The text of each edition should be distilled into a single file of no more than 3,000 to 4,000 characters, and uploaded to the NPTN STUDENT NEWS NETWORK on the nearest system, where it will be distributed automatically to other schools across the network.
Contact: Judson Elliott (aa695@cleveland.freenet.edu)

IDITAROD -
[Multiple grade levels; Special Event - March]

Get the latest reports on the exciting dog sled race across Alaska. Willoughby Middle School brings these reports to you in March as it happens. You can read it on the newsgroup or in your e.mailbox via a listserv.
Contact: Willoughby Middle School (aa695@cleveland.freenet.edu)

SPOTLIGHT ON PEOPLE and SPOTLIGHT ON AUTHORS -
[Multiple grade levels; On-going project]

These projects spotlight accomplished people in all walks of life. Students have an opportunity to write to these people and ask questions. This gives students an opportunity to gain knowledge about leaders, inventors, authors, and various professionals. It also gives accomplished people the ability to

tell the students what they might do to succeed in life.
Contact: Sheryl Maxsom (aj615@yfn.ysu.edu) and Carol Hyatt (chyatt@cap.gwu.edu)

SONNET-WRITING CONTEST -
[Middle and high school students; Special Event - March]

Students are invited to participate in a sonnet writing contest with a panel of impartial literary teachers doing the judging. Cash prizes were awarded in 1993, and will be awarded in 1994. All sonnets are posted to the Student Author newsgroup and then printed in a booklet available from NPTN at cost.
Contact: Marge Cargo (mcargo@eis.calstate.edu)

A DAY IN THE LIFE OF A STUDENT -
[All grade levels; Special Event - January]

Tell others about a day in your life. The project involves keeping a chronological account of a single pre-arranged day from wake-up to bedtime. Student entries can be compiled into a class file and shared with other participants. Classes compare student responses, attitudes and schedules to learn about other types of schools and other cultures.
Contact: Sheldon Smith (shsmit@eis.calstate.edu)

INTERNATIONAL e.CLUB -
[All grade levels; On-going project]

The e.Club is a place where electronic addresses can be exchanged between students (and teachers) who would like to engage in an electronic mail project or simply find a "keypal". We will use this area for exchanging information about the holidays and about the schools during selected special events.

INTERNATIONAL HOLIDAY EXCHANGE -
[All grade levels; Special Event - November to January]

Students around the world can compare their holiday customs. This is a real eye-opener and learning experience as students not only share their favorite customs, but recipes, and reasons behind what makes this such a special time of year.

STUDENT ARTIST -
[All grade levels; On-going project]

This is an area where kids can post their pictures created with word processing programs. This is one of the best ways to reach the youngest kids (and the ESL students), and introduce them to those "extra characters" on the keyboard, while easing them into the world of telecommunications. The older students have successfully presented their holiday greetings as pictures in this area.

Armadillo

From Armadillo, the Texas Studies Project gopher, comes this file about their project area, followed by the menu under Super Projects.

About Super Projects!!!

The Super Projects!!!/ directory will contain work by Texas Students. The theme will generally be Texas Studies in the broadest sense.
If you have projects you would like to have included in Super Projects!!!/ send a description of the project to: armadillo@chico.rice.edu

URL: gopher://riceinfo.rice.edu:1170/1

gopher riceinfo.ricr.edu

Other Gopher and Information Resources/
    Armadillo/
        Super Projects

Super Projects!!!

1. About Super Projects!!!
2. COSN K12 Internet Projects/
3. Class Projects to Share/
4. The CityLink Gopher (Experimental)/
5. A Day in the Life/
6. Distance Education Projects/
7. Folktales/
8. From Russia with Love/
9. Global Handshake Survey (Northbrook MS, SpringBranchISD,TX)/
10. History Projects/
11. Holiday Recipies and their Stories/
12. International Ecology Art Project/
13. Language and Art Projects/
14. Livefrom/
15. Marine Biology Collaboration - Galveston Bay/Chesapeake/
16. Math Projects/
17. Myths and Legends About Texas/
18. Networked Projects /
19. OWLink Distance Education Project/
20. Physical Education Projects/
21. Science Projects/
22. Simulations/
23. TENET Bits and Bytes (From Pat Cook and her SpringBranchkids)/
24. Technology/
25. Transportation/

AskERIC

URL: gopher://ericir.syr.edu:70/11/

gopher ericir.syr.edu

> Other Education Resources/
> Internet Projects for K-12

> Internet Projects for K-12

1. Arkansas Public School Computer Network/
2. Carleton University/
3. Classes wanted for Internet Projects K-12 (via Okla. GeologicalSu../
4. Internet Projects K-12 (via CICnet)/
5. Internet for Minnesota Schools Gopher/
6. MathMagic
7. NCEET/
8. NYSERNet: New York State Education and Research Network/
9. Southern College Gopher
10. University of Massachusetts K12/

CICNet

Here are several examples of projects teachers have used in their classrooms. Many of the projects can be replicated.

URL: gopher://gopher.cic.net:3005/1

gopher gopher.cic.net 3005

> Internet in the Classroom

1. About Classroom Ideas
2. ** How Teachers Find Projects **
3. "Jaunts" Home-town Signs WWW Project
4. "Jaunts" Project Update

5. ASK Prof. Maths (Saint Bonaventure University)
6. Academy One Project List (September 1993)
7. Activities Using Scientific Data CD-ROMs (JEI)
8. Aid to Foreign Language Acquisition
9. Archaeology Units
10. Ask Dr. Math (Swarthmore College)
11. Ask Dr. Science
12. Ask-A-Geologist (US Geological Survey)
13. At-Risk Students
14. Beginning Examples
15. Building a Better Tomorrow
16. CNIDR K-12 Resources (Global Schoolhouse Project, Janice)
17. Chemistry Searches
18. Classroom Programming Projects
19. Cleveland FreeNet and Your School
20. Cloud Study Software from Australia
21. Current Freeware and Shareware
22. Current Issues Project
23. DRUG-OFF program via the Internet
24. Earth Day Treasure Hunt
25. Follow Us (Skiing to the North Pole)
26. Free Environmental Software (EPA)
27. Free Video: Teacher-to-Teacher with Mr. Wizard
28. Global Student Newswire
29. History of Math
30. Internet and Astronomy
31. Introduction to Computer Science for the 21st Century
32. JOURNEY NORTH (Global Study of Spring Migration)
33. KNSO News Service for Jr. High and High School Students
34. Legos on Mars
35. Mail Art Club
36. NASA/AskERIC Multi-media Lesson Plans
37. National Organization of Space Simulating Educators

38. National Student Research Center
39. Online Grammar Hotline (OWL; also available by phone)
40. Student Research Abstracts On-line (NSRC)
41. Telecomputing Activities
42. WhaleNet
43. What's a Sniglet Project
44. What's the Same and What's Different Project
45. Young Kids and Language Arts

COSN

On the Consortium for School Networking gopher there is a menu area listing telecommunications projects including Academy One. Descriptions of the projects and the contact person are given.

URL: gopher://cosn.org:70/11/

gopher cosn.org

Resources on the Network/Educational Resources/
  Network Resources for Education/
    Telecommunications Projects

Telecommunications Projects

1. Current Telecommunications Projects/
2. Earlier Telecommunications Projects/
3. How Teachers Find Projects - A Survey
4. Keys to a Successful Project
5. Stories About Internet Usage in the Classroom - by State/

Global SchoolNet

The Global SchoolNet Foundation organizes, manages, and facilitates projects for schools. They maintain the Global SchoolNet mailing list that updates subscribers about projects, training materials, and special events. Their HILITES archives and mailing list contains a selection of project ideas from previous years. In addition Global SchoolNet provides a mailing list of K-12 schools that have the ability to initiate videoconferencing sessions using the popular software — CUSeeMe. Announcements are made on this list about upcoming events in which schools can participate.

Projects range from videoconferencing to e-mail only. Some sample projects include the Global Schoolhouse, Family Tree-Mail Language Translation using Globalink's language translation software to share family histories in Spanish, French, German, and Italian, and Global Grocery List where students record items and prices on their grocery list then, share that information with partner classes around the world.

URL: http://gsn.org
URL: http://gsn.org/gsn/gsn.projects.html

To subscribe to Global Schoolhouse, address an e-mail message to:
lists@gsn.org
No subject
In the body of the message type:
subscribe global-watch

To subscribe to HILITES, address an e-mail message to:
lists@gsn.org
No subject
In the body of the message type:
subscribe hilites

I*EARN

"The purpose the International Education and Resource Network is to enable participants to undertake projects designed to make a meaningful difference in the health and welfare of the planet and its people." This nonprofit organization creates structured projects that facilitate engaged learning. Project areas include the environment/science, art/literature, social studies/politics, and other interdisciplinary topics. Some examples of student projects are the Holocaust/Genocide Project, the Building Wells for Clean Water in Nicaragua, and Planetary Notions, an environmental newsletter. There is a membership fee to participate.

To find out more information, read about current projects, and view completed projects with evaluations visit their gopher or web site.

URL: http://www.igc.apc.org/iearn

gopher gopher.igc.apc.org

Education and Youth/
    International Education and Resource Network (I*EARN)

K12Net Projects

K12Net is a newsgroup network with an area open for projects called Channels. Here are examples of some of the projects that have been posted. The Project Coordinator for this area is Helen Sternheim.

uucp: uunet!m2xenix!puddle!321!109!Helen.Sternheim
Internet: Helen.Sternheim@f109.n321.z1.fidonet.org

Brown Bag Science

Brown Bag Science Experiments use simple materials and can be sent home with your students. For upper elementary and middle school students.

Global Village News

Community or School News items. These should be articles that have a local flavor. We would enjoy hearing from all areas of the world.

Kidlink

URL: gopher://kids.duq.edu:70/11/

gopher kids.ccit.duq.edu

Kidlink in the Classrooms/
  KIDPROJ Activities How to Set One Up -Currentties Activitties/

1. _
2. KIDPROJ Master Index File   [KIDPROJ MASTER]
3. How To Set Up A KIDPROJ Project   [KIDLINK PROJINFO]
4. Description of projects for 1994-95 [KIDPROJ PROJ95]
5. Everything you want to know about the U.N. [KIDPROJ UN]
6. Lesson Plans for the UNICEF Project/
7. Information on the Transpolar 1994 Expedition/
8. The Desert and Desertification Project/
9. Ham Radio Projects/
10. The Multi-Cultural Calendar/
11. SSCA Shipwreck Project/
12. Writer's Corner Project/
13. Math Penpals Project/
14. Project: What's in a Name?/
15. KIDZINE

MathMagic

MathMagic is an innovative K12 project that involves teams of students solving problems. Every three weeks a new set of problems are posted for different grade levels. It is a majordomo mailing list project sponsored by the MathMagic Foundation. There is no cost to subscribe. There is a nominal fee to participate as a registered user. For more information send a message to:

mail-server@forum.swarthmore.edu
send mathmagic_info

URL: http://forum.swarthmore.edu/mathmagic

NASA

NASA has several initiatives with education. One of these is interactive projects utilizing distance learning, telecommunications, and collaborative efforts within the scientific community.

URL: gopher://quest.arc.nasa.gov:70/11/

gopher quest.arc.nasa.gov

NASA K-12 Interactive Projects

1. Live From..Antarctica (December 94)/
2. FOSTER On-Line (May - June 94)/
3. Live From..Other Worlds (December 93 - February 94)/
4. Women of NASA (January 95 - Presently under Construction)/
5. White Paper on Lessons Learned (Oct 1994)/

STEM~Net   Newfoundland and Labrador

This gopher is under construction, but the French and Science areas provide some nice resources. Under Science you will find project ideas for each grade level.

URL: gopher://info.stemnet.nf.ca:70/11/

gopher info.stemnet.nf.ca

K12 Curriculum and Teaching

1. Primary/
2. Elementary/
3. Intermediate/
4. Enterprise Education/
5. French/
6. Math/
7. Science/
8. Small Schools/
9. Social Studies/
10. Technology Education/

Science Fairs

1. Information About Science Fairs Gopher/
2. Central Newfoundland/
3. Eastern Newfoundland/
4. Email Addresses for Newfoundland Science Fair Councils/
5. Primary Project Ideas.wp5
6. Elementary Project Ideas.wp5
7. Junior High Project Ideas.wp5
8. Senior High Project ideas.wp5
9. The Total List of Ideas.wp5
10. Science Fair Resources/

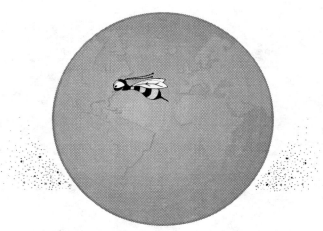

CHAPTER 9

Pointers to
Lesson Plans

Pointers To Lesson Plans

This section gives pointers to lesson plans on the Internet. As new sites are created and more K-12 educators use the network, the potential for curriculum resources will grow.

AskERIC

AskERIC has the most comprehensive collection of lesson plans on the Internet. One of the best features of this site is that you can search by keyword. Access the daily CNN newsroom guide, find a lesson in one of many curricular areas from Big Sky Telegraph, or browse the different menus.

URL: gopher://ericir.syr.edu:70/11/

gopher ericir.syr.edu

AskERIC/
   Lesson Plans

Lesson Plans

1. Search AskERIC Lesson Plans <?>
2. Astronomy: Curriculum Unit for Intermediate Elem. Students/
3. CNN Newsroom Daily Lesson Plans/
4. The Discovery Channel / The Learning Channel/
5. Language Arts/
6. Liquid Crystal
7. Mathematics/
8. Miscellaneous/
9. NASA's SIR-CED Education Program/
10. Newton's Apple Educational Materials/
11. School Library Media Activities Monthly/
12. Science/
13. Social Studies/
14. Lesson Plans from the MVNWR (Minnesota Valley National Wildlife Re../
15. Misc. Lesson Plans & Curriculum Units (from StemNet)/
16. Television and Violence (from SchoolNet)/

BBN's - National School Network Testbed

Lesson plans about the sun pose interesting questions for exploration. You will also find pointers to some multi-user (virtual reality) servers for education.

URL: gopher://copernicus.bbn.com:70/11

gopher copernicus.nnb.com

BNN's/
    National Schools Network Testbed/
        Shadows Science Project
        USCD Internet Lesson Plans
        MUSEs (Multi-user Simulation Environments) in education

Shadows Science Project

1. Earth Stopped Rotating.
2. Path of the Sun.
3. Sun and Angles.
4. Shapes of Shadows.
5. Sun Go Down on the Horizon.
6. Sun Set In the Same Place?.
7. What is Solar Noon?.
8. When Will the Sun Explode?.

UCSD InternNet Lesson Plans

1. About this collection.
2. Biology/
3. Earth Science/
4. English/
5. Lessons in Spanish/
6. Mathematics/
7. Physical Science and Chemistry/
8. Physics/

MUSEs (Multi-user Simulation Environments) in education

1. The MUSE as an educational medium.
2. MicroMuse at MIT.
3. Virtual... Communities, and Informal Science Ed - Barry Kort.
4. MUSE Manual Version 1.5 revision C/
5. Access to educational MUSEs <TEL>

EE - Link National Consortium for Environmental Education

EE-Link provides lesson plans related to environmental issues. The recycling information is very good for projects and reports.

URL: gopher://nceet.snre.umich.edu:70/1
URL: http://www.nceet.snre.umich.edu/

gopher nceet.snre.umich.edu

Activities/Lesson Plans for EE - Link

1. Solid Waste Activities (Cornell)/
2. 18 EE Activities (Big Sky Telegraph BBS and ERIC)/
3. Franklin Science Center (note grade 2 recycling mat'l)/
4. Ozone Hole Teaching Resources from Blue-skies/
5. Project Learning Tree/
6. Recycling: Correspondence Course/
7. Wildlife Lesson Plans (MN Valley Nat'l Wildlife Refuge)/

Eisenhower National Clearinghouse

ENC has an online catalog that you can search to find curriculum materials in math and science. They also point to other math and science related items which are available through the Internet.

URL: gopher://enc.org:70/1

gopher enc.org

Additional Curriculum Resources & Materials/
    Lessons, Activities, Projects/

Mathematics

1. Math Teaching Archives (U.Tennessee)/
2. MathMagic/
3. CHANCE Project (Probability)/
4. Interactive Mathematics Text Project/
5. Visual Math Institute Projects & Materials/

Science

1. NASA Science Resources/
2. Joint Education Initiative (JEI) Archives/
3. Measuring Up (National Res.Council)/
4. Introduction to Computational Fluid Dynamics (CFD)/
5. NASA FOSTER Project/
6. Wolf Study Project (InforMNs)/
7. Dinosaur Unit (InforMNs)/
8. Blue Skies Curriculum Materials/
9. Live From...Other Worlds/
10. San Diego Supercomputer Center Education Outreach Program/
11. Oak Ridge National Laboratory Projects/
12. Women in Science (Kensingon Acad.)/
13. Black Scientists and Inventors (Kensington Academy)/
14. Gaia Crossroads Project/

Galileo

Galileo is an electronic lesson plan distribution and discussion list for science teachers in grades K-12. It is managed by a computer program named Majordomo. To command the Majordomo program, send an e-mail message to: MAJORDOMO@UNR.EDU with one of the following commands in the body of the message:

help - gets a list of all Majordomo's commands
info galileo - gets this page
who galileo - gets list of Galileo subscribers
get galileo index.all - gets an index and description of Galileo lessons
get galileo <filename> - gets a file listed in index.all
subscribe galileo your@address - adds your name to the mailing list
unsubscribe galileo your@address - deletes you from the mailing list

One of the basic premises of science and research is also a value of Galileo: that is, to share lessons, findings, and opinions of K-12 science teaching with others. To communicate with other Galileo subscribers, send an e-mail message to: GALILEO@UNR.EDU. Majordomo will translate the name Galileo and automatically send a copy of your message to each subscriber.

If you would like to submit a lesson plan for consideration, send it via e-mail in ASCII text format to: galileo-approval@unr.edu

Subscribing lets you automatically receive messages posted to the list. You do not have to subscribe to get the index and lesson plans. You can periodically get the index.all file for updates.

INFORMNS (Minnesota K-12 Project)

The Minnesota Valley National Wildlife Refuge provides lesson plans for elementary and secondary students on Wildlife related topics in preparation for visits to their facilities.

URL: gopher://informns.k12.mn.us:70/1

gopher informns.k12.mn.us

Minnesota K-12 Resources/
  Minnesota Valley National Wildlife Refuge/
  Lesson Plans from MVNWR

Elementary Level Lesson Plans from MVNWR

1. 02 Looking for Lifestyles
2. 03 Pond Web
3. 06 Animal Masquerade
4. 07 Birds, Beaks and Adaptations
5. 08 Deer Tails and Trails
6. 09 Eco-Beaver
7. 10 Endangered Species
8. 11 Hunters of the Night
9. 12 Snow Stories
10. 13 The Right Bite
11. 14 Wetland Birds And Their Habitat
12. 17 Mist Netting

Secondary Level Lesson Plans from the MVNWR

1. 05 Snow Pits
2. 16 Soil Shakedown
3. 19 Marsh Dilema
4. 21 Muskrat Marsh
5. 23 White-tails in the Valley
6. 24 Wildlife Telemetry
7. Aquatic Tolerance
8. Biodiversity Game

Kidlink

On November 28, 1989, the Convention on the Rights of the Child was passed by the United Nations. These lessons allow students to think and debate about issues relevant to themselves as children.

URL: gopher://kids.duq.edu:70/11/

gopher kids.ccit.duq.edu

Kidlink in the Classrooms/
  KIDPROJ Activities How to Set One Up - Current Activities/
    Lesson Plans for UNICEF Project

Lesson Plans for the UNICEF Project

1. _.
2. Lesson Plan File Index   [KIDPROJ UNICEF].
3. Introduction   [KIDPROJ UNICEF-A].
4. Lesson 1: Child Rights Convention   [KIDPROJ UNICEF-B].
5. Week 1: Introduction Supplementary   [KIDPROJ UNICEF01].
6. Week 2: KIDS and WATER   [KIDPROJ UNICEF02].
7. Week 3: KEEP US SAFE   [KIDPROJ UNICEF03].
8. Week 4: WE ARE WHAT WE EAT   [KIDPROJ UNICEF04].
9. Week 5: STREET KIDS   [KIDPROJ UNICEF05].
10. Week 6: HEALTH AND EDUCATION   [KIDPROJ UNICEF06].
11. Week 7: CHILDREN WITH DISABILITIES   [KIDPROJ UNICEF07].
12. Week 8: DEVELOPING COUNTRY FOCUS [KIDPROJ UNICEF08].
13. Week 9: GLOBAL ENVIRONMENT   [KIDPROJ UNICEF09].
14. Week 10: Review   [KIDPROJ UNICEF10].
15. KIDS IRC Lesson Experiences/

NASA SpaceLink

For years, NASA SpaceLink has provided teachers with resources about the space program. Astronomy is one topic you can choose from the many on this network.

URL: http://spacelink.msfc.nasa.gov

gopher spacelink.msfc.nasa.gov

Instructional Materials/
   Curriculum Materials/

Astronomy

1. Astro.Companions   [17Jul91, 12kb]
2. Astronomical.Keydates/
3. Astronomy.Classroom.Activities/
4. Astronomy.Classroom.Information   [15Feb93, 25kb]
5. Black.Holes   [17Jul91, 15kb]
6. Comet.Shoemaker-Levy9/
7. ExInEd.Electronic.PictureBooks   [29Sep94, 4kb]
8. How.Big.is.the.Universe   [17Jul91, 10kb]
9. NASA.Foster.Online.K-12/
10. Our.Solar.System/
11. Space.Astronomy.Update/
12. Space.Science.Shorts/
13. Stars.Pulsars.and.Black.Holes   [17Jul91, 5kb]
14. The.Night.Sky/

Scholastic Network

On the Scholastic Internet Gopher, there are many examples of lesson plans from *Instructor* and pointers to other wonderful resources. The libraries can also be searched. Here are some of the menu screens from this service.

URL: gopher://scholastic.com:2003/11/

gopher scholastic.com 2003

Scholastic Internet Libraries

1. READ ME
2. What's in the Libraries
3. Integrating Technology Library/
4. Middle School Science Library/
5. Reading and Language Arts Library/
6. Seasonal Library/
7. Mini-Libraries/
8. Fair Use and Copyright/
9. How to Subscribe: Site License
10. Keyword Lists/
11. Search All Libraries <?>

Language Arts Lesson Plans

1. Books Take You Places
2. Bridge to Terabithia
3. Good-bye, My Wishing Star
4. Grandfriends
5. How My Parents Learned To Eat
6. Number the Stars
7. Songololo
8. The Jolly Postman
9. The True Confessions of Charlotte Doyle
10. What's the Difference?
11. When I Was Young in the Mountains

Notes

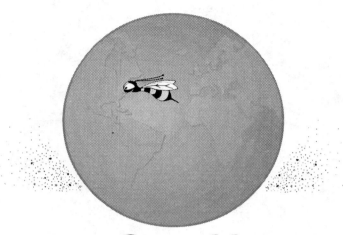

CHAPTER 10

Staff
Development

TRAINING WORKSHOPS

For an article describing how to plan and construct a training model, read *Off We Go Cybernetting - Staff Development Makes the Difference* in the March/April, 1995 issue of *Multimedia Schools*.

Online, Inc.   Phone: 203-761-1466
462 Danbury Road
Wilton, CT 06897-2126

Road Show:

Think about creating a "Road Show" to demonstrate the power of the Internet. You can pull pictures, sounds, and menu screens from the Internet, then use a computer program such as Persuasion or Power Point to show these resources to your audience. If a dedicated telephone line exists at your presentation location, go live online showing e-mail, gopher, or the World Wide Web. Remember to keep the demonstration simple, since your viewers may be new to the concept of the Internet.

Videos:

You may also want to utilize video resources to introduce the Internet to school staff.

Teaching With Technology: Merging Onto the Information Highway

The North Central Regional Educational Laboratory produced this one hour video for educators addressing these topics: access, funding, professional development, and applications in the K-12 curriculum. Printed materials are packaged with the video. It is available at no charge to schools and institutions within NCREL's seven-state region (Indiana, Illinois, Iowa, Michigan, Minnesota, Ohio, and Wisconsin). Licenses for the program are $100 outside NCREL's region. Taping rights are included in the licensing agreement, and they encourage sites to tape the program for their professional development libraries and future use.

NCREL Region: 703-571-4700
License Coordinator
North Central Regional Educational Laboratory
1900 Spring Road, Suite 300
Oak Brook, IL 60521-1480

Outside the NCREL Region: 703-739-5402
PBS K-12 Learning Services
1320 Braddock Place
Alexandria, VA 22314-1698

Global Quest

Global Quest is a fast paced 12 minute video showing how teachers and students are using the Internet in their classrooms. Printed materials accompany the tape. This video may be freely copied and distributed for educational uses. There are three channels of distribution:

1. Regular and frequent broadcasts on NASA Select TV. Gopher to spacelink.msfc.nasa.gov for scheduling.

2. Free duplication at the nearest NASA Teacher ResourceCenter or Regional Teacher Resource Center.

3. NASA's Central Operation of Resources for Educators (CORE) will mail a copy for $18.50, which is the cost plus shipping and handling. More information is available by calling or writing.

Phone: 216-774-1051, x293   Fax: 216-774-2144

NASA CORE
Lorain County Joint Vocational School
5181 Route 58 South
Oberlin, OH 44074

Workshop Timeline

Here is a guide when preparing to conduct a hands-on workshop — the topics to cover and the approximate time to spend on each one.

Day 1:	8:00 A.M. - 11:00 A.M.	Time:
	Introductions:	10 minutes
	Overview of the Internet (Road Show or Video)	15 minutes
	E-mail demonstration	30 minutes
	E-mail hands-on worksheet, signature file	30 minutes
	Break	15 minutes
	Demonstration of gopher and bookmarks	30 minutes
	Hands-on gopher bookmarking	45 minutes
	Wrap-up	5 minutes
Day 2:		
	Welcome, participants check e-mail	25 minutes
	Demonstration of Veronica search	30 minutes
	Hands-on Veronica search	35 minutes
	Break	15 minutes
	Demonstration of downloading & settings	30 minutes
	Hands-on downloading text and picture files	40 minutes
	Wrap-up	5 minutes

Day 3 or a follow-up workshop should include the World Wide Web. The following pages are worksheets to help you better understand how to navigate the Internet. These worksheets were designed to be used with a dial-up shell account or gopher system. They are also adaptable to the Internet tools software.

231

E-MAIL WORKSHEET

To send e-mail using the UNIX system or ELM type the following:

Step 1. At the system prompt >   **m** [mail]
Step 2. To: **userid@domain**
Step 3. Subject: topic for discussion
Step 4. Cc: address of a person you want to receive a carbon copy or press return for none

Step 5. Compose message
Step 6. **control-e**, then **s** for send

The VMS mail system uses a different addressing style:

Step 1. At the system prompt >   **m**
Step 2. To: **IN%"userid@domain"**
Step 3. Subject: topic for discussion
Step 4. Cc: address of a person you want to receive a carbon copy or press return for none

Step 5. **control-z**

Pine e-mail system is menu driven:

Step 1. At the main menu   **c** for compose and send message
Step 2. To: **userid@domain**
Step 3. Cc: address of a person you want to receive a carbon copy or press return for none

Step 4. Attchmnt: filename to send with the e-mail message
Step 5. Subject: type the topic for discussion
Step 6. **control-x**

1. Send an e-mail message to yourself, a participant in the class, or the instructor.

2. Which e-mail system did you use?

FINGER WORKSHEET

FINGER STEP-BY-STEP INSTRUCTIONS:

Step 1. At the system prompt > **finger userid@host**

      [ex. finger ljoseph@magnus.acs.ohio-state.edu]

1. Initiate a finger session from one of the addresses below.

➤   copi@oddjob.uchicago.edu
➤   quake@geophys.washington.edu
➤   nasanews@space.mit.edu
➤   magliaco@pilot.njin.net
➤   aurora@solar.uleth.ca
➤   forecast@typhoon.atmos.colostate.edu

2. Which address did you choose?

3. What kind of information was provided?

GOPHER WORKSHEET

1. Gopher to one of the sites below.

Step 1. At the system prompt > **gopher internet address**

      Example: **gopher copernicus.nnb.com**

If you are already using a gopher system, point to the site and press return.

      Example:

—>   1. AskERIC/

Internet Address	Host
copernicus.nnb.com	BBN'S
cosn.org	Consortium for School Networking
ericir.syr.edu	AskERIC
gopher.cic.net	CICNet
tiesnet.ties.k12.mn.us	Best of K-12
mlink.hh.lib.umich.edu	Go MLINK

2. Which site did you choose?

3. List three resources you found at this gopher site.

WITHIN A **G**OPHER **P**ROGRAM

1. Set a bookmark at: Searching Gopherspace Using Veronica by following this path: Other Gopher Servers/North America/USA/General/AskERIC/Gophers and Libraries/All Gophers/Search gopherspace using Veronica

2. Set a bookmark at: Art and Images at Texas Tech University, Computer Sciences by following this path: Other Gopher Servers/North America/USA/Texas/Texas Tech University, Computer Sciences/Art and Images

3. Using the Veronica search bookmark, point to a Veronica server and search a topic of interest in your curriculum area.

4. Select a text file either from a Veronica search or from one of the gopher exploration sites.

5. Set your telecommunications program for an ASCII text transfer using one of the tranfer protocols. Download and print a text file related to your curriculum area.

6. Using the Art and Images bookmark, go to Animals, Plants, and Scenic Beauty at Indiana University. Point to a GIF image.

7. Set your telecommunications program for a binary file transfer using one of the transfer protocols. Download the image file. View and print the image using your GIF program.

TELNET WORKSHEET

GENERAL TELNET STEP-BY-STEP INSTRUCTIONS:

Before initiating a telnet session make cetain you are at the system prompt.

Step 1. > **telnet internet address** [ex. telnet spacelink.msfc.nasa.gov]
Step 2. login: type the login password   [ex. visitor]
Step 3. TERM= (unknown) > **VT100**   [terminal emulation]

If your screen freezes or you are unable to exit a telnet host, you can escape. To escape telnet:

        1. type ^]   control-right bracket
        2. telnet> **q**

    There may be other steps depending on whether or not the system requires registration.

1. Initiate a telnet session from one of the addresses below:

➢	cap.gwu.edu	login: guest password: visitor
➢	newton.dep.anl.gov	login: bbs
➢	freenet.carleton.ca	login: guest
➢	pac.carl.org	login: pac
➢	yfn2.ysu.edu	login: visitor
➢	ukanaix.cc.ukans.edu	login: history

2. Which telnet site did you choose?

3. Give an example of the information that was available at that site?

World Wide Web Worksheet

1. Start your web browser and go directly to one of the sites listed below. Set a bookmark so you can return to the site at a later date.

Lynx

Step 1. To go to a specific site, type **g**.
Step 2. At the **URL to open:** prompt, type the address.

```
URL to open:http://www.enc.org
```

Netscape

Step 1. Go to File in the Menu Bar and highlight Open Location.
Step 2. Type in the URL address and click on open.

> http://quest.arc.nasa.gov
> http://www.best.com/~mddunn/cybrary
> http://www.c3.lanl.gov/mega-math/welcome.html
> http://www.scholastic.com
> http://volcano.und.nodak.edu/

2. Which site did you choose?

3. Describe how you might introduce or use the information you found with your students.

HTML WORKSHEET

1. Insert the tags in the following document that would create this view on the screen.

                                                    Internet Workshop

                        Welcome to Buckeye Valley School

About Buckeye Valley School
AskERIC

Yahoo Directory

_____

_____

_____Internet Workshop_____

_____

_____

_____ _____Welcome to Buckeye Valley School_____ _____

_____

_____buckeye.html_____About Buckeye Valley School_____

_____

_____http://www.ericir.syr.edu_____AskERIC_____

_____

_____http://www.yahoo.com_____Yahoo Directory_____

_____

_____

ANONYMOUS FTP WORKSHEET

ANONYMOUS FTP SESSION STEP-BY-STEP INSTRUCTIONS FOR TEXT FILE:

Before initiating an ftp session make cetain you are at the system prompt.

Step 1. > **ftp internet address**　　[remote host] [ex: ftp ftp.loc.gov]
Step 2. Name (internet address of the host: userid) **anonymous**
Step 3. Password: **your name@host** [ex: jdoe@magnus.acs.ohio-state.edu]
Step 4. ftp> **dir**
Step 5. ftp> **cd directory name**　　[ex: cd pub]　or
　　　　ftp> **cd /dir/dir/dir**　　　[ex: cd /pub/research.guides
Step 6. ftp> **get filename**　　　　[ex: get WWII.bib]
Step 7. ftp> **bye**　　　　　　　　[exits remote host ftp site]
Step 8. > **ls or dir**　　　　　　　[lists files in your home
　　　　　　　　　　　　　　　　　　　directory]
Step 9. > **more filename**　　　　　[view text file on a Unix system]

1. Intiate an ftp session to one of the sites below:

Host cs.dal.ca

　　Location: /comp.archives/sci.research
　　　　FILE -r—r—r—　　 2374 Sep 15 1991 locating-grants-information

Host grasp1.univ-lyon1.fr

　　Location: /pub/nfs-mounted/ftp.univ-lyon1.fr/usenet-stats/groups/info
　　　　FILE -rw-r—r—　　 582 Jan 2 16:50 info.nsf.grants

Host ftp.luth.se

　　Location: /pub/misc/lyrics/folk/t
　　　　FILE -rw-r—r—　　 2509 Oct 22 1992 the_first_of_the_emigrants

Host life.anu.edu.au

Location: /pub/general/fun
    FILE -rw-rw-rw-   16105 Jun 8 00:00 whitehouse.faq

Host sunsite.unc.edu

Location: /pub/academic/political-science
    DIRECTORY drwxr-xr-x   512 Jan 4 16:10 whitehouse-
                                  healthcare.archive
    DIRECTORY drwxr-xr-x   512 Jan 1 22:06 whitehouse-papers

Host byrd.mu.wvnet.edu

Location: /pub/history/internet
    FILE -rwxrwxr—   18949 Oct 7 21:14 whitehouse_email.txt

Location: /pub/yeager
    FILE -rwxrwxr—   16182 Sep 9 10:52 whitehouse.txt

Host nic.sura.net

Location: /pub/nic
    FILE -rw-r—r—   17797 Jul 7 00:00 whitehouse.FAQ

2. Transfer a file from the host to your account

3. What Internet site did you choose?

4. What file did you choose for transfer?

5. Give a brief summary of the information contained in the file.

Digging For Net Nuggets

Navigating the Internet can lead to great sources of information that can be utilized in many creative ways with students. Find the answer to each of the following questions, making certain to write down the steps or path which led you to it. Have fun digging for those golden net nuggets!

For example:

Where would I find information about Zora Neale Hurston?

> Archie search using the word Hurston
> anonymous ftp seq1.loc.gov
> path: /pub/Library.of.Congress/research.guides/amer.folklife.ctr
> file: Hurston.findingaid

1. My students are doing reports on countries. Where would they find general information on population, government, and other statistics?

2. My students are preparing for the annual science fair. This year they would like to query scientists about information on their project topic. Can the Internet help?

3. Where is Cripple Creek?

4. Where can I find the daily news about NASA?

5. I would like my students to communicate with keypals in other states or countries. Where can I find keypals or penpals?

6. I desperately need a new lesson plan for teaching current events as well as some video clips to go along with it. Do you have any suggestions?

7. I teach in a French immersion school. I would like my students to find things on the Internet using their French language skills. Where can I find a K-12 French gopher?

8. The daily drill and practice can get old in my math class. With all the material we are required to cover, I have little time to dream up creative projects. Is there a K-12 network group with project ideas?

9. Our foreign language students are planning a trip to Germany. Where can we learn about the currency exchange?

10. My students are writing their own fables. Are there fables on the Internet they could read?

Bonus Question:
Where can I find a list of words for "Welcome" in different languages?

Notes

CHAPTER 11

Acceptable Use

Acceptable Use Policy

Internet Ethics were established to ensure the reliable operation of the Internet and the responsible use of its resources. In RFC 1087 (Requests for Comments), the Internet Advisory Board endorsed the Division Advisory Panel of the National Science Foundation Division Network, Communications Research and Infrastructure, which paraphrased as unethical and unacceptable any activity that purposely:

(a) seeks to gain unauthorized access to the resources of the Internet,

(b) disrupts the intended use of the Internet

(c) wastes resources (people, capacity, computer) through such actions,

(d) destroys the integrity of computer-based information, and/or

(e) compromises the privacy of users

Connect to InterNic to find the full text of this document along with other Internet infrastructure files. The *Net User Guidelines and Netiquette* can be found at Florida Atlantic University.

gopher rs6000.adm.fau.edu

World Wide Gophers/North America/USA/Florida Atlantic University/

    Computing Information/
      Internet Documentation/

URL: gopher://rs6000.adm.fau.edu:70/11/Computing%20Information/
Internet%20Documentation

Child Safety on the Information Highway

http://www.describe.ca/childfind/infohwy.hte

The National Center for Missing and Exploited Children and the Interactive Services Association have jointly sponsored a 12 page brochure about the benefits and risks of the information highway. Written by Lawrence J. Magid, it addresses guidelines and online safety rules for parents and students. The print version is available from the National Center for Missing and Exploited Children at 1-800-843-5678.

School Use

With the privilege to use the Internet comes responsibility. School Districts generally set up guidelines or standards for students accessing the Internet from their buildings. These are referred to as acceptable use policies or technology codes of conduct. Both parents and students are required to sign the agreement. By signing the agreement, students take on the responsibility for their actions while on the Internet.

Following is one policy example. There are several other examples you can read or download from the Internet. Here are two locations for acceptable use policies:

gopher ericir.syr.edu

Internet Guides and Directories/
    Acceptable Use Policies/
        Agreements for K-12

gopher chico.rice.edu 1170/11/

Armadillo/
    More About Armadillo and Other Gophers/
        Acceptable and Unacceptable Use of Net Resources (K12)

Example of Acceptable Use Policy from NuevaNet for the Nueva School:

NuevaNet Acceptable Use Policy
The Nueva School

NuevaNet MISSION STATEMENT

NuevaNet is service provided by and in consonance with the dual mission of The Nueva School:

Mission I: To enhance innovative education for gifted and talented children through access to unique resources and collaborations;

Mission II: To improve learning and teaching through research, teacher training, collaboration and dissemination of successful educational practices, methods, and materials.

NuevaNet is connected to the Bay Area Regional Research Network (BARRNet) which in turn connects it to the Internet. The Internet links computer networks around the world, giving NuevaNet access to a wide variety of computer and information resources. In general, electronic traffic passes freely in a trusting atmosphere with a minimum of constraints.

NuevaNet provides open access to these local, national and international sources of information and collaboration vital to intellectual inquiry in a democracy. In defining the Internet's resources as an extension of the Library, this network subscribes to the Library Bill of Rights which states that "A person's right to use a library should not be denied or abridged because of origin, age, background or views."

In return every NuevaNet user has the responsibility to respect and protect the rights of every user in our community and on the Internet. NuevaNet account holders are expected to act in a responsible, ethical and legal manner, in accordance with the Nueva Code of Conduct, the missions and purposes of the other networks they use on the Internet and the laws of the states and the United States.

NuevaNet ACCOUNT HOLDERS

A NuevaNet account is a privilege offered each academic year to the following:

1. All students at Nueva, prekindergarten through grade eight, and their parent(s) or guardian(s).

2. All educators who are working with Nueva students, including classroom teachers, support personnel, administrators, tutors, music staff, specialists and mentors.

3. Educators and students from other educational institutions who are working in partnership with The Nueva School for specific purposes over a limited period of time.

NuevaNet CODE OF CONDUCT

NUEVA's Code of Conduct applies to all users of NuevaNet. It reads:

"I will strive to act in all situations with honesty, integrity and respect for the rights of others and to help others to behave in a similar fashion. I will make a conscious effort to be of service to others and to the community. I agree to follow Nueva's basic rules: no killer statements, no damage to property, and no violence."

The NuevaNet account holder is held responsible for his/her actions and activity within his/her account. Unacceptable uses of the network will result

result in the suspension or revoking of these privileges. Some examples of such unacceptable use are:

1. Using the network for any illegal activity, including violation of copyright or other contracts;

2. Using the network for financial or commercial gain;

3. Degrading or disrupting equipment or system performance;

4. Vandalizing the data of another user;

5. Wastefully using finite resources;

6. Gaining unauthorized access to resources or entities;

7. Invading the privacy of individuals;

8. Using an account owned by another user;

9. Posting personal communications without the author's consent;

10. Posting anonymous messages.

NuevaNet CONSENT AND WAIVER

By signing the Consent and Waiver form attached, the requestor and his/her parent(s) or guardian(s) (if the requester is a student) agree to abide by these restrictions. The student and his/her parent(s) or guardian(s) should discuss these rights and responsibilities together.

Further, the requestor and his/her parent(s) or guardian(s) are warned that The Nueva School does not have control of the information on the Internet, nor does it provide any barriers to account holders accessing the full range of information available other than those constraints imposed by finite resources. Other sites accessible via the Internet may contain material that is illegal, defamatory, inaccurate or potentially offensive to some people.

While NuevaNet's intent is to make Internet access available to further its educational goals and objectives, account holders will have the ability to access other materials as well.

Nueva believes that the benefits to educators and students from access to the Internet, in the form of information resources and opportunities for collaboration, far exceed any disadvantages of access. But ultimately, parent(s) and guardian(s) of minors are responsible for setting and conveying the standards that their child or ward should follow. To that end, Nueva supports and respects each family's right to decide whether or not to apply for NuevaNet access.

The account holder and, if a minor, his/her parent(s) or guardian(s) must understand that NuevaNet is an experimental system being developed to support Nueva's educational responsibilities and missions. The specific conditions and services being offered will change from time to time. In addition, an account holder uses NuevaNet at his/her own risk. Nueva makes no warranties with respect to NuevaNet service, and it specifically assumes no responsibilities for:

1. The content of any advice or information received by an account holder from a source outside Nueva, or any costs or charges incurred as a result of seeing or accepting such advice;

2. Any costs, liability or damages caused by the way the account holder chooses to use his/her NuevaNet access;

3. Any consequences of service interruptions or changes, even if these disruptions arise from circumstances under the control of Nueva;

4. While NuevaNet supports the privacy of electronic mail, account users must assume that this cannot be guaranteed.

THE NUEVA SCHOOL

NuevaNet Consent and Waiver Form

NuevaNet is a local area network connected to other local and national networks such as the Bay Area Regional Research Network and Internet ("Independent Networks"). In furtherance of its educational mission and in order to enhance its students' access to educational resources The Nueva School permits its staff, students and their parents, and others collaborating with Nueva on educational endeavors access to NuevaNet and other Independent Networks.

Prior to receiving a NuevaNet account, an individual must read, understand and consent to the following conditions:

1. NuevaNet and other Independent Networks may contain information or material which may be offensive and/or unsuitable for minors or adults. As Nueva does not control or monitor information accessible on Independent Networks, the undersigned agrees to discharge and hold harmless the School, its officers, trustees and employees from any and all claims, liabilities, demands, causes of action, costs, expenses or obligations of any kind, known or unknown, arising out of or in any way relating to his/her own or his/her child's use of or access to NuevaNet or the Independent Networks, except as provided by California Labor Code, section 2802.

2. The undersigned acknowledges that Nueva's Code of Conduct applies to the use of NuevaNet and Independent Networks, and that any usage of these networks in violation of this code or the School's policy and procedures regarding usage of the networks will be subject to appropriate disciplinary action, including but not limited to loss of NuevaNet privileges. If a problem escalates, Nueva's conflict resolution process will be followed.

3. Nueva would like to emphasize that the Independent Networks, accessed through NuevaNet, are open systems. This means that another individual

within or outside the Nueva community might access a NuevaNet user's files without the user's prior knowledge or consent. Therefore, Nueva's advice to all NuevaNet users is "Don't put anything in writing that you wouldn't want other people to read. "

As it is impossible to guarantee complete security, Nueva accepts no responsibility for any consequences of unauthorized entry, even if such entry could have been prevented by procedures known to Nueva but not adopted.

4. Nueva will make reasonable efforts to protect the electronic files of every account holder. However, an account holder's files may be reviewed, collected and/or used by Nueva:

    a. As required by law
    b. As a part of system maintenance activities
    c. When there is reason to believe an account is being used for improper or illegal use
    d. With the permission of the account holder

Applicant Name (please print clearly):

_____

(Please: we must receive a separate form for each applicant)

Account category: ___pre-K   ___K   ___1-2   ___3-4
                   ___5-6   ___7-8
                   ___staff   ___parent   ___alumnus
                   ___other:_____

Address:_____

_____

_____

Phone: (_____)_____

Please indicate your consent by signing on the appropriate line(s) below:

Signature of Applicant: _____

Date:_____

Signature of Parent/Guardian: _____

Date:_____
(if Applicant is under 18, both Applicant and a Parent
or Guardian must sign)
—————————————————Do not write below this line———————————————

UID assigned:_____Password: _____

Date Entered:_____ Processed by: _____
*NuevaNet Acceptable Use Policy, including Nueva's Code of Conduct
accompanies this consent and waiver form.

Notes

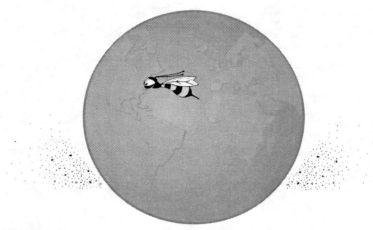

CHAPTER 12

Troubleshooting

TROUBLESHOOTING

PROBLEM:

POSSIBLE SOLUTIONS:

1. No dial tone

- Make certain all cabling is connected.

- Make certain the phone cable is plugged into the wall socket of the modem.

- The phone should be plugged into the modem versus the modem plugged into the phone.
Phone -> Modem -> Wall Plug

- Call the telephone company to check the line.

2. No Carrier

- You are disconnected from the service, try again.

3. Phone rings but the host does not answer

- Host is not working properly, try again later.

4. Garbage characters on the screen

- This could be telephone line noise, try again.

- Check to see if the baud rate is set correctly.

5. Burst of errors, then lose connection

- Try deactivating call waiting *70 then the number

6. Electrical interference	• Disconnect a cordless phone.
7. Menu looks strange and items are not displayed correctlty	• This is probably a terminal emulation problem. Make sure the setting is correct. VT100 is the most common.
8. Closed by foreign host	• There are too many connections, try again later.
9. Login seems okay, but host responds with unauthorized user	• Try again, perhaps you hit the wrong key. • You must be a registered user with a valid ID.
10. Screen freezes	• Try typing control-c • Try typing control-] • Disconnect and redial.

Glossary

Analog - signals used in voice or music. These are continuous signals sent over telephone lines.

Baud Rate - the rate at which data is transmitted over a telephone line. 300, 1200, 2400, and 9600 bps (bits per second) are commonly used.

Bit - the most basic unit of data that can be recognized by a computer, either a 0 or a 1.

Client - software running on your workstation transferring information to and from a server.

Browser - software program used to search the World Wide Web.

Data Bits - ASCII (American Standard Code for Information Interchange) defines 128 different characters that can be used for data transmission. Another 128 characters were added by computer manufacturers, making a total of 256 characters which may be transmitted. 7 binary digits (bits) are needed for 128 characters and 8 binary digits (bits) are needed for 256 characters.

Demodulate - conversion of an analog signal to a digital signal.

Digital, binary - a signal that is comprised of a 1 or 0, either on or off. It is not continuous.

Download - transferring a file from the host computer to your computer.

Duplex - refers to whether data can flow in two directions at the same time (full duplex) or one direction at a time (half duplex). Most modems are full duplex.

E-MAIL - electronic mail sent from one person to another via computer.

FAQ - frequently asked questions.

Finger - a program that examines a person's login file.

Flame - critical remark made by someone about something posted on a news or discussion group

FTP - File Transfer Protocol is a function that allows the user (client) to get files from a remote computer (host).

Gopher - a menu driven program that will automatically make ftp and telnet connections to global networks.

Gopherspace - all the information that is available through gopher.

Host Computer - the computer which holds the database or bulletin board often times called the server.

HTML - the language used to create a hypertext document on the World Wide Web.

http - hypertext transfer protocol used on the World Wide Web.

Hytelnet - a menu driven system that initiates a telnet session for the user.

Internet Address - the series of numbers or letters that identifies the site of the host computer. The suffix of the address often helps the user know what kind of service they are connected to on the network. Internet addresses are used for ftp, telnet, gopher, and e-mail. Example: Heartland Free-Net: heartland.bradley.edu (136.176.5.114).

ISDN - Integrated Services Digital Network offers a higher speed — between 64 and 128 kbs — on a dial-up connection.

IP - Internet Protocol.

Jughead - allows the user to search a limited area of gopherspace, such as the gopher server at a specific university.

Listserv - a discussion group focused on a particular area of interest; subscribed to via e-mail.

Lurker - someone who subscribes to a discussion group, but does not participate. Some groups sponsor unlurking days.

MIME - Multipurpose Internet Mail Extension. An extension to an e-mail program that allows the transfer of non-text data such as graphics.

Modem - a piece of hardware that acts as a translator between computers and telephone lines.

Modulate - conversion of a digital signal to an analog signal.

MUD - Multi-user domain; online virtual reality.

MOO - Object oriented MUD.

Newbie - someone new to the Internet.

OPAC - Online Public Access Catalog. Library catalogs that have been computerized.

Parity - basically a primitive form of error checking between computers. The settings can be even, odd, mark, space, or none. Normally error checking is not used and parity is set to none.

RFC - Request for Comments document.

Server - software that allows the host computer to offer up information.

SMTP - Simple Mail Transfer Protocol. The Internet standard for transferring electronic messages from one computer to another.

Spam or Spamming - stuffing someone's mailbox with the same message numerous times, which causes their mail system to crash; or posting a lengthy message to the whole group that should be sent directly to an individual. Mailbombs.

Stop Bit - marks the end of a character. 1 stop bit is the standard.

T1 - a high speed line at 1.544 mbs.

T3 - a high speed line at 44.736 mbs.

TCP - Transmission Control Protocol.

Telnet - a program that connects the user to a host computer with an interactive welcome screen. Telnet sessions allow the user to view information on a host computer as though the user were sitting at its terminal.

Terminal Emulation - allows the client (user) computer to communicate with the host computer in the same language.

Under Construction - a term used for areas that are being built or revised.

Upload - transferring a file from the client (user) computer to the host computer.

URL - Uniform Resource Locator. It is also an address for the World Wide Web.

Veronica - allows the user to search and find topics in gopherspace.

WAIS - Wide Area Information Server. Allows the user to search a database by keyword.

WHOIS - a searchable directory of people and their Internet addresses.

WebMaster - the person who maintains a World Wide Web server.

Notes

BIBLIOGRAPHY

Baker, Christopher, et. al. *Telecommunications Handbook Connecting to Newton.* Argonne, IL: Argonne National Laboratory, 1992.

Eisenberg, Michael B. and Robert E. Berkowitz. *Information Problem-Solving: The Big Six Skills Approach to Library & Information Skills Instruction.* Ablex Publishing Corporation: Norwood, NJ: 1990.

Eisenberg, Michael B. "Internet Capabilities in an Information Problem-Solving Context." *Educational Technology;* v34 n7 Sept. 1994, p.63.

Eisenberg, Michael B. and Robert E. Berkowitz. *Resource Companion to Curriculum Initiative: An Agenda and Strategy for Library Media Programs.* Ablex Publishing Corporation: Norwood, NJ: 1988.

Estrada, Susan. *Connecting to the Internet.* Sebastopol, CA: O'Reilly & Associates, Inc., 1993.

Farley, Laine. ed. *Library Resources on the Internet: Strategies for Selection and Use.* Chicago: American Library Association, 1992.

Hahn, Harley and Rick Stout. *The Internet Complete Reference.* Berkeley: Osborne McGraw-Hill, 1994.

Hahn, Harley and Rick Stout. *The Internet Yellow Pages.* Berkeley: Osborne McGraw-Hill, 1994.

Internet Resource Directory for Educators. [Online] Available: FTP: tcet.unt.edu Directory: pub/ telecomputing-info/IRD Files: IRD-ftp-archives.txt, IRD-infusion-ideas.txt, IRD-listservs.txt, IRD-telnet-sites.txt

Kehoe, Brendan K. *Zen and the Art of the Internet.* 2nd ed. Englewood Cliffs: Prentice Hall, 1994.

Krol, Ed. *The Whole Internet Catalog and User's Guide.* Sebastopol, CA: O'Reilly & Associates, Inc., 1992.

Lane, Elizabeth and Craig Summerhill. *An Internet Primer for Information Professionals.* Westport, CT: Meckler, 1993.

LaQuey, Tracy. *Internet Companion.* New York: Addison-Wesley Publishing Company, 1993.

Li, Xi. and Nancy B. Crane. *Electronic Style: A Guide to Citing Electronic Information.* Westport, CT: Meckler, 1993.

Yanoff, Scott. *Special Internet Connections.* [Online]. Available: FTP: alpha2.csd.uwm.edu Directory: pub/ File: inet-services.txt

Notes

INDEX

SmartPages™ from Greyden Press.
Providing Your Company

with

Customer
Awareness that
Spans the Globe.

SmartPages™ unites your targeted advertising message with the powerful technology of the Internet by utilizing highly visual and interactive World Wide Web Home Pages.

Imagine having your sales message accessible by any business or home computer. SmartPages™ puts you online with over 30 million Internet subscribers, and offers you the capability to deliver a multimedia presentation at a fraction of the cost of conventional advertising.

There are three SmartPage products from which to choose. Call today and we'll be glad to rush you additional information on the future of marketing and advertising via Internet, the Information Superhighway.

Call 800/881-9421
E-Mail: info@zip.com
Http://www.smartpages.com

Greyden Press
2020 Builders Place
Columbus, OH 43204
614/488-2525
Fax: 614/488-2817

Do You Need To Have a Book, Manuscript, or Document Printed?
Would You Like To Have It Digitally Stored For Future Use?

If So, GREYDEN PRESS Is As Close As Your Internet Connection...

We're Only An FTP* Away!

GREYDEN PRESS
The Custom Publishing People

Announcing a **NEW** *and* **EASY** *way to* **INTRODUCE** *young minds to the* **INTERNET**.

WORLD LINK

An Internet Guide for Educators, Parents, and Students

by Linda C. Joseph

Have you wondered . . .

* How do I connect to the Internet?
* What software do I need?
* What is Gopher, Telnet, and World Wide Web?
* How can I use the Internet in my curriculum?

World Link answers these questions and many more.
It's your **complete step-by-step guide** to the
Information Superhighway.
